T0087761

# Crazy Busy

## Keeping Sane in a Stressful World

Thijs Launspach

CAPSTONE
A Wiley Brand

This edition first published 2022

Copyright © 2022 by Thijs Launspach. All rights reserved.

Originally published as Fokking druk: Het ultieme anti-stressboek by Uitgeverij Unieboek | Het Spectrum bv in 2018.

All rights reserved. No part of this publication may be reproduced, stored in a retrieval system, or transmitted, in any form or by any means, electronic, mechanical, photocopying, recording or otherwise, except as permitted by law. Advice on how to obtain permission to reuse material from this title is available at http://www.wiley.com/go/permissions.

The right of Thijs Launspach to be identified as the author of this work has been asserted in accordance with law.

*Registered office*
John Wiley & Sons, Inc., 111 River Street, Hoboken, NJ 07030, USA

John Wiley & Sons Ltd, The Atrium, Southern Gate, Chichester, West Sussex, PO19 8SQ, United Kingdom

Wiley-VCH GmbH, Boschstr. 12, 69469 Weinheim, Germany

John Wiley & Sons Singapore Pte. Ltd, 1 Fusionopolis Walk, #06-01 Solaris South Tower, Singapore 138628

*Editorial Office*
John Wiley & Sons Ltd, The Atrium, Southern Gate, Chichester, West Sussex, PO19 8SQ, United Kingdom

Boschstr. 12, 69469 Weinheim, Germany

1 Fusionopolis Walk, #06-01 Solaris South Tower, Singapore 138628

For details of our global editorial offices, customer services, and more information about Wiley products visit us at www.wiley.com.

Wiley also publishes its books in a variety of electronic formats and by print-on-demand. Some content that appears in standard print versions of this book may not be available in other formats.

Designations used by companies to distinguish their products are often claimed as trademarks. All brand names and product names used in this book are trade names, service marks, trademarks or registered trademarks of their respective owners. The publisher is not associated with any product or vendor mentioned in this book.

*Limit of Liability/Disclaimer of Warranty*
While the publisher and authors have used their best efforts in preparing this work, they make no representations or warranties with respect to the accuracy or completeness of the contents of this work and specifically disclaim all warranties, including without limitation any implied warranties of merchantability or fitness for a particular purpose. No warranty may be created or extended by sales representatives, written sales materials or promotional statements for this work. The fact that an organization, website, or product is referred to in this work as a citation and/or potential source of further information does not mean that the publisher and authors endorse the information or services the organization, website, or product may provide or recommendations it may make. This work is sold with the understanding that the publisher is not engaged in rendering professional services. The advice and strategies contained herein may not be suitable for your situation. You should consult with a specialist where appropriate. Further, readers should be aware that websites listed in this work may have changed or disappeared between when this work was written and when it is read. Neither the publisher nor authors shall be liable for any loss of profit or any other commercial damages, including but not limited to special, incidental, consequential, or other damages.

*Library of Congress Cataloging-in-Publication Data is Available:*

ISBN 9780857089458 (Paperback)
ISBN 9780857089472 (ePub)
ISBN 9780857089465 (ePDF)

Translation: Danny Guinan
Cover design: Eric Huijsen / Moker Ontwerp
Photography: Nanda Hagenaars
Original illustrations: Elgraphic

Set in SabonLTStd 11/14pt by Straive, Chennai, India SKY10036378_100622

# Crazy Busy

# Contents

# Contents

Contents

# Introduction

Given the incredibly hectic lives we lead today, is it even possible to find enough time to relax and unwind? Can you reduce the amount of stress you experience without your life becoming boring? How can you avoid a burnout while staying productive at the same time?

Meetings, deadlines, breaking news, e-mail notifications, social media updates, a thousand consumer choices per day, our free time filled to the brim with social activities – the life we lead nowadays can be incredibly busy. And we seem to like it that way. We like to feel productive. We value hard work. We enjoy our leisure activities. All things considered, we regard a busy life as a good life.

There may not be a lot wrong with leading a busy life, if you're able to manage the excesses and find ways to recover from the busyness, that is. If you're not careful, however, being 'nicely busy' can easily tip over into being 'crazy busy'. And if you're crazy busy all of the time, this can lead to all kinds of trouble: exhaustion, anxiety and even burnout.

Burnout is a huge and growing problem. Approximately half of all employees in the US say they experience dangerously high levels of stress because of their work. In the UK, one in five employees complains of being on the verge of burning out because they are no longer able to handle the pressure of work. For certain groups (women, 25 to 35-year-olds, people who work in the health care sector or in education) these numbers are even higher. In the UK, one in three of all cases of absenteeism are directly related to burnout.

While your body and mind are quite able to process normal day-to-day stress, prolonged stress can result in you suffering a burnout. Up until quite recently, complaints related to stress and burnout were often dismissed as nonsense. We considered burnout to be something that only ever affected perfectionists who were unable to handle the 'normal' pressure of work. People who suffered from stress were thought of as 'weak' and labelled as drama queens. Fortunately, we now know better: given how busy our lives are these days, everyone is a potential victim of burnout. And that's all down to the way in which we live and work.

Not only are the people who burn out are feeling the heat. Even if you never reach the burnout stage, an excess of stress can easily diminish your quality of life. This 'everyday' kind of stress can cause you to enjoy life less and pay too little attention to others. It can make you feel like you are a slave to the machine. It can give you the feeling that you are always playing catch-up and are never on time with your work, a bit like the White Rabbit in Alice in Wonderland who is always 'too late!' Stress has a negative effect on how you interact with others and it makes you less outgoing. It prevents you from being fully present in the moment because your mind is always elsewhere. And in the long term, stress can lead to many negative health outcomes, such as heart problems.

In other words, a high level of stress often comes at a very high price.

There is no need to let it come to that, however, and there are a number of basic principles you can use to prevent stress from ruling your life. Of course, it is impossible to avoid stress completely – it's a simple fact of life – but this does not mean you are condemned to suffer interminably from its slings and arrows. There are plenty of things you can do to minimise the effect busyness has on your life and to prevent excessive levels of stress. And you don't have to wait until the last moment, either, before intervening. You can take steps now that will prevent you from falling victim to stress. You don't have to be wealthy or privileged to be able to enjoy a more relaxed life and experience less stress. Nor does your life have to become boring. It is possible to be as productive as you have always been and to enjoy doing interesting things, but then with a much lower level of stress.

Beating stress requires a bit more effort than engaging in a few wellness sessions, drinking cups of chamomile tea and taking out a subscription to Happiful Magazine (although all of these can help, too). If you want a more peaceful life, you might need to rethink the way you live and work. There are a couple of adjustments, techniques and exercises that can help you to deal with the inevitable stress in your work and life. And this book will show you how to use them.

My interest in the subject of stress is not purely academic. Stress has been a recurring theme in my own life, too. Unlike many of my friends and colleagues I (touch wood) have never suffered a burnout. Like many of us, however, I have had periods in my life where stress affected me in negative ways. I wasn't much fun to be around. I felt overwhelmed, anxious and depressed. My mind was always preoccupied with work. I lashed out frequently at the people closest to me. The busier I was, the shorter my fuse became. Sometimes I failed to notice what was going on right in front of my nose because my mind was simply miles away. Stress put an enormous strain on my relationship with family and friends. It spoiled holidays, too, because I would spend them running around like a headless chicken. In the past, stress has turned me into a less likable person on more than one occasion. This, I felt, was not the way I wanted to live my life.

While researching the material for this book I read countless studies and publications. I also spoke with many experts in the areas of stress and burnout. And I even subjected myself to some rigorous self-study. I attempted to cure my Facebook addiction. I made drastic changes to the way in which I work (and the way I think about work). I signed up for a mindfulness trainer programme. I hired a personal assistant to see what effect that would have on my stress levels. I even took Ritalin to find out how it would affect my concentration. In an attempt to banish stress I tried different kinds of yoga, learned how to slow my heart rate down with the help of breathing techniques and signed up for different types of massages and wellness treatments (hard work, I know, but someone's got to do it).

What I found out was this: learning how to cope with stress is not rocket science. The most effective ways of dealing with stress are, in fact, pretty self-evident. They involve listening to what your body tells you, setting priorities for yourself and being able to say 'no' when required. It's all about finding the right balance between availability and rest, about training your attention and working more efficiently. The challenge lies not so much in knowing what you should do, but in maintaining consistency in how you do things: how do you take care of yourself while people are constantly demanding something from you? In order to manage the stress in your life, you need to take care of yourself first, even if others are demanding your attention. The choice for a less busy life is yours and yours alone, but to be able to make that choice you need to be armed with sufficient self-confidence and self-knowledge.

In this book we will examine the 'stress problem'. Which aspects – of our work, our personal life and our mind – cause stress? Why do we feel the need to be busy every waking moment of the day? How have we come to accept a busy life as the normal state of affairs? We will examine what stress is exactly, what constitutes a burnout and what you can do to deal with the stress in your life. The book also contains lots of tips on how to prevent stress and boost your concentration and attention. These tips will help you to bring more calm to your life and relieve stress. Take it from me: all of this can make your life a lot more enjoyable.

When you are reading this book you may sometimes have to pause and think about how it applies to your own specific situation. In places I may use the word 'he' where I could just as easily have used 'she'. Remove and replace as you see fit.

You will also encounter the phrases 'your work' or 'your job' frequently, while you may in fact be your own boss or still a student. I also use the word 'task' regularly to describe everything from a conversation with a client or writing an article to performing a surgical procedure. Feel free to use the words and phrases that best suit your own situation.

Remember, you are the one who decides how to live your life. And how you manage the stress in your life is your choice, too. But if you don't choose, others will force their decisions upon you. If you're unable to make the hard choices, you will be left with a diary that is permanently full to bursting, an eternally hectic life and a perpetual feeling of haste. I cannot guarantee that after reading this book your life will be completely free of stress. But I can promise you that the tips in this book will help you handle stress more effectively. Not a bad prospect, really, considering how crazy busy we all are these days.

# 10 Ways to Lower Your Stress Levels – A Quick Guide

Okay, great, a book that will help you to deal with stress, but chances are that right now you don't have the time to read a whole book about how to live a more relaxed life. So, to start with, here are a few tips that will help you to quickly lower your stress levels; a kind of first aid kit for stress. These tips summarise the main ideas addressed in the individual chapters in the book. To explore the tips in more detail, you can go straight to the relevant chapter.

## 1. Take care of yourself (sleep, eat, rest)

Do you get enough sleep and at the right times? Do you eat well? Do you get enough exercise? Do you have enough time to relax, to 'switch off'? If you answer 'no' to any of these questions, you need to change your lifestyle. Your physical fitness has a major effect on how you feel. If you don't take care of your body, you will automatically experience more stress than when you are rested and fit. That's why one of the first steps when tackling stress is: take good care of your body, especially when you feel like you don't have the time to do so.

(Chapter 6: Warning!; Essential maintenance)

## 2. Just breathe

Breathing, you do it all day long. However, by becoming more conscious of how you breathe you can lower your stress level in a matter of minutes. Breathing deeply slows down your heart rate and lowers your blood pressure, which results in a less troubled mind. You can delay or even eliminate your stress response simply by doing a few breathing exercises. It helps just to breathe calmly in through your nose and out through your mouth for a few minutes. For a deeper form of relaxation try breathing in less frequently but more deeply using the 4-7-8 technique: inhale for four seconds, hold your breath for seven seconds and exhale for eight seconds. Sounds simple, but it works like a charm.

(Chapter 4: Your Boss is a Bear; Breathe)

## 3. Turn off all notifications on your devices

One of the main sources of stress is the many different devices we use throughout the day. Our telephones, laptops and tablets overload us with information, even when we're not looking for it. Once you receive a notification it will stay in your head until you do something with it – that's just the way our brains are wired – including when you are busy doing something else. Turning off all notifications will result in fewer interruptions, less switching and consequently less stress. You will still have access to all the information, but only when you decide to access it yourself.

(Chapter 2: Always in a Hurry; The dictator in your pocket)

## 4. Check your e-mail no more than three times a day

Research has shown that people who check their mail only three times a day are happier, more efficient and less stressed than people who check their e-mail continuously throughout the day. This suggests that you can cut your stress level dramatically simply by checking your mail less often: for example, early in the morning, after lunch and at the end of the day. Let's be honest, before the invention of e-mail no one spent the entire day in the hall waiting for the post to drop through the door.

(Chapter 1: We're All Workaholics Now; The terrible tale of e-mail)

## 5. Recognise and react to warning signs

Stress does different things to different kinds of people. While one person may suffer headaches, another will experience pain in their neck and shoulders. Others have trouble sleeping or feel like they are always in a hurry. Some become cynical or develop a temper. It is essential that you learn to recognise your own warning signs and react appropriately when required. It is only when you know how stress affects you that you can react in an effective manner.

(Chapter 6: Warning!; Recognising your warning signs)

6. **Keep your head as empty as possible**

What things are currently fighting for attention inside your head? Most of us have a lot going on in our minds at any given moment. If there are too many bits of information demanding your attention, it can result in a permanent kind of background noise, like when there are too many tabs open in your internet browser. With a mind full of stuff it's easy to get overwhelmed. So, to avoid descending further into chaos, it is a good idea to keep your head as empty as possible. Train yourself to write down things that occupy your mind instead of storing them in your memory. The emptier your head, the more space you will have for the stuff that really counts.

(Chapter 2: Always in a Hurry; Organising stuff)

7. **Plan like a boss**

There is a lot more to planning than simply making a list or adding dates to a calendar. A good plan involves creating an overview, setting priorities and making sure the most important things always get done. Ideally, it allows you to concentrate fully on whatever you are doing at the moment. And that helps immensely when it comes to keeping a clear head.

(Chapter 7: Peace of Mind; Planning for professionals)

## 8. 'Good enough' is good enough

Stress is often the result of feeling overwhelmed by your work. This is especially true if you happen to be a perfectionist: it is impossible to do everything perfectly and extremely quickly at the same time. Try experimenting with lowering the bar in terms of what you demand of yourself. Chances are that others will not even notice – if you're a perfectionist, your personal standards are probably a lot higher than what others generally expect from you. 'Good enough' is good enough: this is true more often than you might think.

(Chapter 3: Being Busy is a Choice; Perfectionism)

## 9. Train your attention

When the pressure is on it is essential that you can concentrate on whatever happens to be your top priority at that particular moment. In these days of constant distraction, being able to focus your attention is like a superpower. Luckily, there are ways to train your ability to focus. Mindfulness exercises can be a great help. Here's one simple exercise: go to the window and sit and stare outside for ten minutes. When you find yourself becoming distracted by your own thoughts, refocus your attention on whatever it was you were looking at.

(Chapter 8: Focused on the Job; Mindfulness)

## 10. Do NOTHING more often

If you're not careful, your week will have filled itself in the blink of an eye with important, enjoyable and interesting things to do. And if you feel you have no choice but to stick to all those plans – even when you have neither the energy nor the inclination to do so – you will soon end up in trouble. Try experimenting with the noble art of cancelling stuff. You don't have to stick to your appointments simply because they are in your diary. It's okay to cancel things, as long as you do this diplomatically and in a timely manner. And who knows, the other person might be just as relieved as you are when you do. . .

(Chapter 6: Warning!; Taking action)

# 1
# WE'RE ALL WORKAHOLICS NOW

Back in the 1930s the economist John Maynard Keynes had a vision. He predicted that in the future we would only have to work 15 hours a week. At the time, technology was changing fast and much of the manual labour was being taken over by machines, with the result that the same amount of money could be made in less time and with a lot less effort. Where workers once needed a whole day to complete a certain task, it now only required a few hours of their time.

This meant that workers would no longer be required to spend most of their day in the factory, Keynes reasoned, and they would have more time left over for the really important stuff: relaxing, studying, spending time with their families and generally enjoying life.

This prediction did not turn out to be entirely correct, however, and we all know what happened instead. Factory owners discovered that the opportunity to scale up using the same number of workers meant that they could actually produce more. They expanded their factories and invested in modern machines. They split the production process up into smaller tasks and gave workers the responsibility for one of those tasks. Workers went from being makers of products to just cogs in a machine, responsible for a single sub-task in a much larger production process. As a result, goods began rolling off the conveyor belt at lightning speed and productivity went through the roof. And the poor workers? They were condemned to working increasingly longer shifts, raising their production goals and dealing with micromanaging oversight. Instead of enjoying more free time, they ended up working even longer hours.

Today we are facing a similarly momentous change in the way we work: a digital revolution. Only 20 years ago the internet was the exclusive domain of nerds who dialled into the network using a modem. Now we are all connected to the web – and that has major implications for almost every aspect of our lives. The internet has changed work drastically. Messages are sent and received in the blink of an eye. Everyone is online and available all of the time. You don't even need to be on the same continent, never mind in the same room, as other people anymore in order to collaborate – a fact that entire industries were quick to embrace during the COVID crisis. In the modern era, you can work at any time of the day or night you like. But there are also drawbacks, such as the blurring of the line between your personal and professional life (especially when 'working remotely' from your own couch or bedroom) and the many extra hours of work you put in as a consequence.

The West is becoming more of a knowledge economy, as the actual production of goods continues to be farmed out to countries where the cost of labour is low. At work we now use our hands sparingly, but our minds all the more. Much of our time is spent on managing information. For many people, work involves staring at a computer screen for a significant portion of their day. Even the more traditional professions (teachers, plumbers, care workers) are becoming more digital.

The digital revolution was supposed to make our lives more relaxed and more enjoyable, at least that was what they promised us. However, just like the previous period of great change – the industrial revolution – things haven't exactly worked out the way we thought they would. In fact, our lives have become more complex and busier than ever before, as our jobs have become more demanding. The increasing amount of time we devote to our work is often at the cost of the hours we could be spending on other things, such as family and friends and caring for others. No wonder we are now more restless and stressed out than ever before.

Which is not to say that our attitude towards work hasn't changed. Nowadays, we rarely have factory managers or snarky supervisors bossing us around. Mostly, we actually like our work, at least to a certain extent. It is the source of our sense of purpose and self-worth. You are what you do, and that is why we work long and hard. But if you're not careful, work can become addictive as well and you can end up living in order to work, instead of the other way around.

Work, like other addictions, can actively harm you and those around you as well.

In the 80s and 90s there was a word for people who worked too much: workaholics. The tell-tale signs of workaholism included devoting an extraordinary amount of time to work and being preoccupied with it even when not working, all to the detriment of other activities in your life. Today the term 'workaholic' has all but vanished from our vocabulary. However, I don't think that's because workaholism itself has disappeared. I think it's because we're *all* inclined to be workaholics now. Being a workaholic has become so normal that it is no longer regarded as strange or out of the ordinary.

In this chapter we will be examining our addiction to work. We will look at those aspects of work that make our lives crazy busy. We will study the major changes that have taken place in the work arena over the past few decades and examine the psychological consequences of those changes.

## #LoveMyJob

If you find yourself striking up a conversation with someone you don't know at a party, the first thing you are likely to ask them after exchanging names is: 'So, what do you do?' Everyone has their own stock answer to this question, and it usually involves our work. My own answer to this inevitable question varies slightly depending on the occasion. Sometimes I say I'm a psychologist, sometimes a trainer or a teacher and sometimes, when I want to sound interesting, I introduce myself as a writer. The person posing the question would probably be very surprised if I said something like, 'Oh, I collect stamps' or 'I eat lots of crackers'. That would be outside the rules of the game.

The fact that we in the West immediately jump to our occupation when introducing ourselves is not surprising. But it is not a universal phenomenon. There are lots of countries and cultures where you wouldn't even mention your job when meeting someone new. You may be more likely to say something like, 'Do you have a family?', 'Where do you come from?' or 'Who are your parents?'

The fact that we in the West like to highlight our career when we meet someone says a lot about how much we value our work. This is not unusual, however, because we often measure our value as a human being in terms of our performance on the work floor. It is our job that gives us status – the amount of respect we are afforded – and naturally we want that status to be as high as possible.

Whereas long ago it was generally assumed that a person who was born poor would remain poor for the rest of their life, today the situation is quite different. We now assume that our position in society is no longer determined on the basis of our social-economic background or status but on the basis of suitability. If you manage to climb the ladder of success, it is not because your parents are rich but because you are smart and work hard – or at least that's the idea. This means that, in theory, everyone can reach the top of the heap if they are clever enough and willing to put in the effort. This idea is central to the myth of the American Dream in particular: with enough dedication and sheer graft, even the penniless paperboy can become a rich and famous media tycoon. (Unfortunately, that's not the whole story. Being successful also requires plenty of good fortune and there are very real limits to what we can achieve based on our ethnicity, gender and background – things that have very little to do with our skills, grit or ability).

Today we are told we can become whatever we want and that we ought to aspire to reaching the very top. We base our self-worth, our confidence and our value as a human being on the achievements in our careers. And we evaluate others according to the same standards as well. We admire those who have already climbed high on the ladder of success and look down on those who are still stuck on the first rung.

Our work is an important part of our identity. It is not just what we do but also what we *are*. Our work is not just one of the many activities we engage in during the week. It is supposed to be our 'passion', the thing that gives us meaning and purpose. And the thing that makes us happy, too, if possible.

According to the philosopher Alain de Botton, this is what characterises working in the twenty-first century more than anything else: the idea that work is a tool for making us happy. This notion, one that we generally accept as being true, is a relatively recent phenomenon. Down through history work was mostly seen as something unpleasant that could not be avoided – almost a kind of punishment ('by the sweat of your brow...'). You traded your time and energy for a fitting reward: a salary. If you had a choice, however, you would much prefer to spend your time doing something else, but because you needed to eat you had to spend your days doing these unpleasant but necessary tasks. Today, however, we are not encouraged to view our work as a necessary evil but as a means towards self-fulfilment. In fact, it is not unusual to speak of work in terms of a 'mission', an opportunity to leave your mark on this mortal coil.

Some people believe that the ideal outcome is finding work that is so gratifying and important we would probably still do it even if we didn't get paid: 'Find a job you love and you'll never have to work another day in your life.' The idea is that once you have found your dream job, the one that meets all of your expectations, it will not feel like a job at all but more like your favourite hobby. #LoveMyJob.

This idea is also evident in the popular management speak of today. We believe it is important to 'make full use of our potential' and 'to get the best out of ourselves'. We engage in 'personal branding' and work on our own 'unique selling point'. We are 'passionate' about our work because it matches our 'core values'. And when our work doesn't quite 'feel' the way it should, we can hire a job coach to help us find a job that is more suited to our needs.

The modern employer is a so-called 'absorptive corporation', an organisation that is prepared to go the extra mile to satisfy its employees' demands. Today, organisations pay a lot of attention to the happiness of their workers (as long as it doesn't tamper with their profit margins). After all, employees turn up each day not only to work but also to socialise. Sporting events and courses are organised on a regular basis and many organisations have their own training academy and a bar for drinks after work. The latest trend is to appoint a Chief Happiness Officer whose job is to enhance the 'employee experience', ensure that workers are happy in their work and offer them coaching when that is not the case.

The result is a further blurring of the line between our professional and private lives. We no longer regard work as a punitive thing; it is the source of our self-confidence and enhances our self-realisation. However, all this meaningful work comes at a considerable price: complete and utter dedication to the cause, even at the expense of our own health.

## Continuous change

It is not only our perspective on work that has changed, but also the actual work we do. Our jobs have also become more digitalised and far more complex. And that's not only true for influencers, coders and webshop entrepreneurs but also for more traditional jobs.

Not so long ago the job of a bicycle mechanic primarily involved repairing bicycles. Today it demands a lot more, such as an understanding of social media marketing, the ability to process a digital order for spare parts, excellent people skills and an up-to-date knowledge of sales techniques to boot.

In secondary school I had a history teacher called Mr Van Dijk who was, shall we say, rather 'old school'. Mr Van Dijk was an excellent teacher because he was very good at two things: talking about history and maintaining order in the classroom. His reputation spread far beyond our own school. When he was giving a lesson about Napoleon, for example, he would turn up dressed in full uniform as the general himself, including his famous hat. If the day's lesson was about Caesar, he would recite Brutus' speech from memory – in Latin. His second skill – maintaining order – was one he was actually a little too good at. First-year students would enter his classroom with their knees knocking. If Mr Van Dijk caught one of them whispering during class, he would physically pick the offender up, chair and all, and dump them in the corridor. Today, other teachers still recall the legendary story of when he first heard a mobile phone going off in his classroom in the late 1990s. He grabbed it from the student and without hesitation flung it out the window.

Mr Van Dijk, who sadly is no longer among us, stubbornly resisted all of the changes in the educational system during the latter stages of his career. He wouldn't allow computers in his classroom or a projector to run PowerPoint presentations. He flatly refused to offer coaching sessions on how to pass exams and ignored the whole concept of project-based learning. He simply told stories and it was up to us to distil the information we required from them.

By the time the most dramatic changes were being made to the educational system, Mr Van Dijk had already retired. Today, computers and laptops are ever-present in the classroom. Teachers give interactive lessons on smartboards and continuously apply the latest developments in educational science. Students do their homework in a digital learning environment. And teachers now have a whole portfolio of other tasks in addition to their teaching requirements: maintaining an up-to-date record of student behaviour in a digital database and coaching students in presentation, teamwork and conflict management skills; sending updates to students and their parents regarding organisational matters; and marking papers, which usually has to be done after school hours (if they can find the time). No wonder the number of stress-related complaints and burnouts is so high among teachers.

Bicycle mechanics and history teachers are not alone in this, of course. Almost all traditional professions have become more complex and demanding in one way or another. Nearly every job description nowadays includes tasks that are not directly related to the position in question. It's often not enough just to be good at your main task in your line of work; you have to be good at organising things, negotiating with others and selling yourself as well. Even artists are required to position themselves in the market nowadays as 'cultural entrepreneurs'.

You could say that many in the working population now have to know how to operate as a project manager in addition to their regular job. It is no longer enough to be armed with the knowledge and expertise required for your profession. We also have to be flexible allrounders who can learn other skills very quickly. It is the only way of keeping up with the rapid developments in technology.

There is nothing wrong, of course, with an ever-changing working environment: it keeps us alert and prevents us from becoming bored. There are lots of people who enjoy having a very dynamic job that requires them to adapt quickly. Some workers value a working environment where no two days are ever the same. But for the majority of people, frequent change is not always a good thing. Too many changes in a short period of time can make you uneasy, insecure and stressed. Having a routine helps you to know where you stand with regard to your work. Constantly having to think about how you should approach a particular task costs a lot of mental energy and leads to higher levels of work-related stress.

## Committed to the cause

In traditional firms and organisations it was up to the manager or team leader to make sure that employees stuck to the rules and delivered sufficient quality. The manager had authority and a direct line to the 'men upstairs', dressed more formally than his[1] workers and had his own office to which the worker was summoned if they did something wrong.

This scenario is hopelessly outdated today. The modern manager is more of a coach or an 'inspirer'. They dress the same as you and I and work in the same office space as the rest of us. In a job performance review, you and the manager discuss whether or not you have achieved the goals you set for yourself. Ideally, your manager regularly checks to see whether you are happy with your place in the team. And if you're not, their door is always open if you want to get any problems off your chest.

So what about the authority that the manager once possessed? That has been passed on to us. The manager no longer has to keep an eye on us because we keep a good eye on ourselves. In fact, you could say that each of us has become our own result-oriented manager. The old-fashioned hierarchical organisation is making way for democratic firms in which we are responsible for our own behaviour. We ensure we make good use of our time (and if we can't, we sign up for a course or two), that we deliver the required level of quality in our work and that we are as productive as humanly possible. If we fail to deliver the desired quality, we feel bad about it. And if, at the end of the day, there is still some work left over, we make sure it gets done, even in our free time. That's how committed we are.

Sam (23) is a student who works part-time for a home care provider in Amsterdam. It is a modern, horizontal organisation employing mainly students who work in self-managing teams. Sam has been working there for almost four years.

She began as a nurse's assistant helping with cleaning, putting on elastic socks and other relatively simple tasks. The longer she worked for the organisation, the more administrative responsibility she was given: intakes with clients, planning and facilitating team meetings and recruiting new staff. She is now a 'team coach' – the organisation prefers not to use the word 'coordinator' because it implies a hierarchical structure. Sam: 'I'm not the boss, and I don't get paid like one, but it is my responsibility to manage the team, give instructions and correct colleagues when they make a mistake.'

In the organisation the carers are more or less their own boss – at least in theory. They decide themselves how to organise the care required by a client, sometimes in consultation with the team coach. In practice, however, they often come to her for instructions. And when something goes wrong it often ends up in Sam's lap. Although her remit includes making sure that the team is self-managing, when there is a problem she is usually the one who ends up having to solve it. Recently, one of the team members had a conflict with a client. The client was so angry that she kept on calling the carer on the phone. 'The carer was very upset and turned to me for help. And it wasn't the first time.'

This kind of situation arises more than once a week. Sam is paid to work four hours a week as a team coach, a task that requires her not only to solve problems for team members but also to organise and chair meetings and train in new carers. The work always takes longer than the four hours allocated. 'When I say that the workload is too heavy I am usually told that I should leave some of the work to the carers. I should make sure that my team is better at managing itself. I need to make the team responsible for solving their own problems and not to come running to me every time. I get told off for taking on the work that the carers should be doing themselves. But if I hand that responsibility back to them, it means they have to do all that extra work for no extra pay. And telling them to look after everything themselves may only end up causing them more stress as well.'

Sam's story illustrates one of the ways in which our work often demands our complete commitment nowadays, even at the expense of our own time. We are prepared to go that extra mile for our work, and sometimes even further. In some professions it is now often more the rule than the exception to carry a work phone with you at all times so that you can be contacted in the evenings and even at the weekend. In other sectors it is completely normal for your job description to include tasks for which you will receive no reimbursement but that you are expected to carry out. I once worked for an employer who expected me to attend a team meeting once a month on an evening during the week without getting paid for my contribution. Everyone regarded this as normal practice.

In the current working climate, a 9-to-5 mentality just won't do anymore. These days you are expected not only to do your job well, meet your deadlines and targets and be a genuine team player. Nor is it enough to be a dedicated and proactive worker during your working hours. You are also expected to put your heart and soul into the job, to make your work your absolute priority – often at the expense of the other things in your life that deserve attention. And the best way to display this deep level of commitment is by taking on the extra work, like when a client has a crisis at ten in the evening or when a colleague falls ill. Pitching in whenever and wherever you are needed has become the norm. And when you're unable to go beyond the call of duty due to illness or other responsibilities, the result is often a feeling of guilt: not only have you let yourself down, but you have also saddled your colleagues with a problem.

## Always on

In the organisation where Sam works there is a lot of communication between staff, particularly via WhatsApp. The amount of information they send each other is sometimes overwhelming. 'We have separate WhatsApp groups for a whole range of things: for the team, for the mentors, personal messages and an emergency app group. We also have a group for a training project for carers that I'm involved in. And then there are the buddy groups, too, in case a carer needs individual support. The list is endless actually.'

It is not always clear whether a message concerns a professional or a personal matter. If it is about a client, then it is work-related, and if one of the staff sends a message to colleagues inviting them to a party, then it is meant as a personal message, that much is clear. However, the distinction is not always obvious: if you are trying to set a date for a company get-together and want to find out when your colleagues are available, should you consider that a professional or a personal matter? If you have had a bad day and you want to vent your frustration to one of your colleagues, should that be regarded as work? The solution is simple: to treat every single message as being both relevant and important.

Only the team coaches where Sam works are given a work phone. The rest of the staff have to use their own phone for work-related matters. Strictly speaking, they are not obliged to give their private telephone number to clients, but that tends to happen in almost all cases anyway.

Despite the fact that Sam has a work phone in addition to her own phone, personal and professional communication often get mixed up. At first she tried keeping all of the WhatsApp groups on her work phone. She endeavoured to keep that phone switched off outside of working hours. As time went by, however, Sam began using her own phone as a kind of back-up: 'It's just not handy having to carry two phones around. Sometimes I missed an urgent message when my work phone was turned off. I wasn't happy about that and decided to have all my messages sent to my personal phone as well. Eventually, all the WhatsApp groups ended up on my own phone – I couldn't handle the stress of possibly missing an important message. Now, however, my phone is constantly bleeping day and night and all through the weekend.' What goes for Sam also goes for many of us: it's often incredibly difficult to disconnect from the flow of work-related information. In a way, communicating has become too easy. There's no added cost attached to communicating with several people at the same time: all you have to do is cc everyone you want to contact in an e-mail. And it only takes two minutes to create a WhatsApp group that can contain an endless number of contacts. We are far from frugal when it comes to sending text messages, mails and DMs. And we seem to accept our constantly overflowing mailboxes and never-ending stream of notifications as a fact of modern life.

Whereas there used to be a clear distinction between working hours and free time, the two now often tend to overlap. The team of lecturers at the university where I work has a WhatsApp group for communicating with each other. The group contains 15 lecturers and is regularly used for questions related to teaching ('Can I borrow a set of markers from someone?') and planning ('The deadline for marking your papers is tonight!'). At the weekends the group app is also used for matters not related to work ('Look who I bumped into last night in the pub!').

A while back one of my colleagues asked a question in the group app on a Sunday morning: 'Just got a mail from a student. She's panicking because she can't find the submission form for the project. Anyone know where to find it?' Within a few minutes a colleague had replied suggesting that it was probably on the website. Not long afterwards came another message: 'Sorry folks, forgot to upload it!! Danny, do you have it handy?' Danny then replied: 'Just mailed it to you!'

In no time this question from a colleague on a Sunday morning had four colleagues back in work mode. Eleven other lecturers had their Sunday brunch interrupted by a string of messages regarding a problem that could easily have waited until Monday.

We often fail to recognise just how much technologies like WhatsApp demand of our time, attention and headspace, and that of others, too. When we send a message we rarely stop to consider whether the intended recipient wants to receive it or not. It doesn't matter to WhatsApp whether or not you want to receive messages about your work during your time off.

And an e-mail never politely asks you if they may have a moment of your time, it just takes it.

WhatsApp messages, mails and other forms of messaging are not subject to the rules of conventional working hours. Before the emergence of the internet and mobile telephones, the average worker was almost never contacted about work-related matters outside of working hours. Some professions, for example dentists and police officers, were always informed in advance when they had to remain contactable 24/7 for a certain period of time. Today, however, the door to the private arena is being kicked wide open in an increasing number of professions. For many, being constantly available has become the norm, including in the evenings and at the weekend. As if work has become a 24/7 phenomenon in itself. In theory, you can delete the e-mail application from your phone or remove the notifications for WhatsApp groups. But can you really permit yourself to do this when it is considered completely normal for you to react to messages from work sent during the weekend?

The norm that determines whether something is important enough for you to contact your colleagues about it is changing. In Sam's case, she regularly receives 'emergency' calls in the evenings and at the weekend. There is no higher authority that regulates the stream of messages and phone calls, no explicit rules governing the times when workers may be contacted. Of course, failing to respond to a message or to answer the phone at the weekend is not something that, normally speaking, will get you fired. Sam: 'But is has become ingrained in our working culture. You feel guilty when you leave a colleague or client to sort out a problem without your help.

I think it's stretching it a bit when we are expected to be 'on call' all week, including at weekends. I try not to answer my telephone after 8 p.m. but sometimes it's unavoidable. And as team coach I am often guilty of contacting colleagues about work after dinner time and in the weekend. I'm as guilty as everyone else of propping up the system.'

Because of our dedication to our work we often allow it (willingly or otherwise) to seep into our personal lives. This results in a problem that often goes unnoticed: the amount of genuinely free time we can enjoy is diminishing, time when we don't feel an obligation to our work. Free time that becomes swallowed by work is not free time at all, it's just more working hours in disguise. Even when you receive a message about work in the evening or at the weekend and decide not to respond to it, it will continue to occupy your thoughts.

## The terrible tale of e-mail

We are mailing ourselves silly. According to recent data, we send each other somewhere between 183 and 205 billion e-mails each day on a global basis. Approximately 75% of those mails are answered within one hour. A study of office workers revealed that the average employee receives between two and three hundred e-mails each day and spends around two and a half hours a day reading and replying to e-mails. Whereas in 2002 less than 10% of workers checked their mail outside of office hours, today that number is almost 50%. Another study showed that the average office worker spends around 13 hours a week processing e-mails. That is 650 hours each year, or 28% of their total working time.

Even though answering e-mails is not part of the job description for the majority of workers, we still spend an enormous portion of our working day doing just that. As a result, our addiction to e-mail is having a significant effect on our productivity. The more time we devote to our mailbox, the less we have left over for other aspects of our work. And when we do get around to paying those other aspects some attention, our inbox just starts filling up again with dozens of mails. Replying to our e-mails also means we are stealing the working time of others – given that the norm is to reply immediately to an e-mail – thereby completing the circle.

E-mail is disastrous for your attention, especially when you are tempted to check your inbox every five minutes. Most e-mail software is designed to capture your attention the moment an e-mail drops into your mailbox. A notification appears on your screen, you hear a sound like a ping or a bell, or a bright red circle appears above an icon. You are tempted to stop whatever you are doing and divert your attention to the incoming mail, and you usually do this immediately. Research has shown that people who turn off their mail notifications switch between computer programmes an average of 18 times per hour, while those whose concentration is disrupted by incoming e-mails switch 37 times per hour.

Humans are not really all that good at multi-tasking. We may think that we are very adept at switching regularly between tasks and still manage to be very productive at the same time, but the truth is that we get a lot less done. In fact, whenever we become distracted and have to refocus on the task we had been performing, it costs us a lot of time and cognitive effort. Studies have shown that after replying to an e-mail we need an average of one minute and four seconds to revert to the previous task. If, for instance, you are busy writing up a plan and an e-mail comes in and you decide to react to it immediately, it will take you more than one minute to refocus your attention again on what you were writing. Do that 30 times per hour and almost all of your writing time disappears.

Each e-mail you receive triggers a new multi-step process in your head, one that you are not always aware of. Out of the enormous pile of e-mails we have to digest each week, on average only 38% can be considered important or even relevant. The first question we ask ourselves when we receive an e-mail is: do I need to respond to this? If the answer is 'yes', this leads to a series of additional questions: how exactly should I respond? What should my next move be? Should I simply respond to the e-mail or does it require some other action, like finding a document? And when should I do that: immediately, later? This process repeats itself with each new e-mail. And each time it eats away at your mental energy, especially when you are in the habit of reacting to your e-mails the moment they appear.

Another drawback of e-mail is that it is often difficult to determine whether a mail is important or not. After all, an e-mail that may be of major consequence to your career looks exactly the same as one inviting you to make a contribution to a gift for your colleague, Sabrina. E-mail does have a system of symbols and flags for marking relevance but they say more about the importance of the mail to the sender and not necessarily to you, the receiver. Often, the only way of establishing the importance of an e-mail is to read it in full.

It is also sometimes difficult to figure out what an e-mail is asking of you, exactly. A clear and intelligible mail is usually very brief and reveals its most important content either in the subject matter or in the first few lines, including how it expects you, the receiver, to react. Unfortunately, a large portion of the mails we receive are far from intelligible and they usually require a comprehensive scan in order to uncover the message. Whereas ideally you should be able to establish whether a mail is relevant or not – and how you should respond – within ten seconds, the poorly composed e-mails we are more used to receiving often take us several minutes to decipher. It will come as no surprise that I am all in favour of severely punishing the senders of unintelligible e-mails.

Why do our mailboxes become so jampacked with e-mails, most of which are actually irrelevant? It's all down to the ease of use and speed of the medium itself. There is almost nothing that stops us from sending an e-mail anymore, with the result that we have become pretty nonchalant about our reasons for sending them. For instance, my students often send me e-mails with questions they could easily answer themselves if they just took the time to Google them.[2] But mailing me is faster, apparently, and I surely won't ignore their request (they think...).

E-mails are often poorly written because of the speed of the medium. An e-mail containing an article and the question 'What do you think of this?' isn't exactly what you would call crystal clear. What kind of response does the sender expect? An e-mail like this often sets off a series of replies back and forth until the original intention of the e-mail has been established. Another common problem with email is the tendency to include more people in the cc than is strictly necessary, simply because you can. With e-mail the motto is often: when in doubt, include as many people as you can think of and hit Send!

It is very easy to waste huge amounts of time on e-mail, especially if you belong to the *Inbox Zero* crowd – those who can only ever sit back and relax when they have dealt with every single mail in their inbox. This is what turns e-mail into a major stress factor at work. If you are a CEO or a distinguished university professor, you can usually get away with not replying to all of your mail (the strategy of these VIPS seems to be: as a rule, don't reply unless you are sent a reminder). However, us mere mortals rarely enjoy this luxury. The norm is to reply to all your e-mails, unless you have a very good reason for not doing so.

For many of us, e-mail is a source of extra work over which we have no control. This can be very stressful when you are inclined to reply to incoming messages as quickly as possible. In fact, e-mail has become a kind of extra to-do list, but then one that is drawn up by others – not exactly ideal in terms of your workload.

In a Canadian study into the effect of e-mail on stress, the participants were monitored for a period of two weeks. A record was kept of how often they checked their e-mail, how stressed they were and their general happiness levels. In the first week they were instructed to behave as they normally would with regard to their e-mail. In that week the participants checked their inbox 15 times a day on average. In the following week they were asked to check their mail three times a day – in the morning, at lunchtime and at the end of the day. The first result the researchers noted was not surprising: participants were unable to stick to the rules. They checked their e-mail an average of five times a day instead of the recommended three. However, this was still far less frequent than in the week when there were no restrictions on how often they could check their mail. The second, more important result was that participants in the study experienced less stress and appeared happier in the week when they had restricted access to their e-mail. It seems that being a little stricter about when you check your inbox can lead to a sizable reduction in your stress levels.

## The need to switch off

Does your work take priority over everything, sometimes even at the expense of your health? If so, you are not alone. Our work provides us with a sense of self-worth and self-confidence, as well as a sense of purpose. It determines our status and is the medium we use to leave our mark on the world. Our work is extremely important to us and that is why we are prepared to put up with the pressure, stress and fatigue that it precipitates.

Generally speaking there's nothing wrong with working hard and displaying your commitment to the cause. But when this is at the expense of your well-being the consequences can be far-reaching. In that case you have no choice but to tackle your addiction to work: to learn how to say 'no' when required, to safeguard your free time, not to answer your work phone outside of office hours and to ignore your e-mail as much as possible. This will allow you to work hard *and* find enough time to unwind.

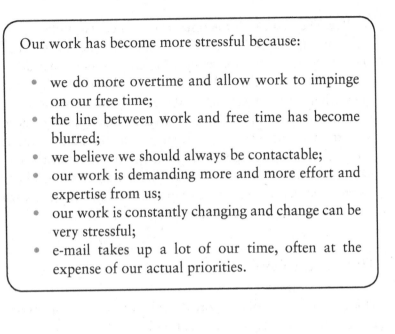

Our work has become more stressful because:

- we do more overtime and allow work to impinge on our free time;
- the line between work and free time has become blurred;
- we believe we should always be contactable;
- our work is demanding more and more effort and expertise from us;
- our work is constantly changing and change can be very stressful;
- e-mail takes up a lot of our time, often at the expense of our actual priorities.

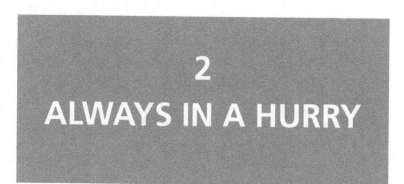

# 2
# ALWAYS IN A HURRY

Imagine you are at home relaxing on the couch. Suddenly, you hear a loud noise outside. When you look out the window you see that a UFO has landed next to your house. A hatch opens and out comes a green alien, who then walks over and knocks on your door. When you open your front door in astonishment the alien says, 'I come in peace. But I need your help.' He explains that for unusual but still plausible reasons he needs to fill his life with as much stress as possible. What advice would you give to the alien?

I often conduct this thought experiment during lectures and workshops. My students usually come up with answers like: 'Give him a telephone and subscribe him to multiple message groups and e-mail lists so that he can be constantly called and receive millions of messages'; 'Tell him to hire a bike and try cycling through the centre of Amsterdam'; or 'Give him a list of unrealistic targets and impossible deadlines and a gigantic to-do list'.

When I dig deeper it doesn't take long before they start to offer the alien the kind of advice that touches on the more fundamental causes of stress in our lives. They coach our green friend on how to strive for perfection and how to blame himself if he doesn't meet his own bloated expectations. And another good way of maxing out the alien's stress levels: constantly comparing yourself with people who are more successful than you and negatively evaluating your own achievements in comparison to theirs.

The most common piece of advice our alien receives is this: to experience severe stress, what you need to do is cram as much of everything into your life as you can, spend most of your time and energy on the wrong kinds of things and be mad at yourself when you fail to meet your own expectations. This is the perfect recipe for filling one's life with an abundance of stress.

Funnily enough, many of us follow the above advice ourselves without batting an eyelid. We believe it is entirely logical to want to 'get the most you can out of life', including during our free time. We are used to having a busy mind, a full diary and a long to-do list. We regularly bite off more than we can chew. Rest and relaxation are not a priority. And whenever our lives are less busy than usual, we feel guilty about it. We aim to squeeze as much as we can out of every minute and are scared to death we might miss out on something important. The obvious consequence of all of this is stress and more stress – and it's no wonder that so many of us fall into this particular trap.

## FOMO

If you're anything like me, then your diary is always full to bursting. Next to my 'regular' job I always have a number of other projects going on the side (writing this book, for instance, or setting up a new business). I also try to squeeze as much as possible out of my free time: playing music, getting enough exercise, reading, meeting up with friends and fitting in a few social visits each week, too. And when I do take a holiday I always have a readymade list of things to do and books to read that I would otherwise never get around to. When I insist on keeping up this high tempo my body eventually decides to protest, my carefully-laid plans all go awry and I have to accept that things are not going to go the way I intended. After the dust has settled I usually find myself wondering: why do I always end up falling into the same trap of wanting too much?

I can barely remember the last time I wasn't busy, and I know I'm not the only one. None of us is exactly modest with regard to what we expect from life. We want to be rich, successful, happy, healthy, creative, fit, attractive and affable, all while leading as interesting a life as possible. If we are not successful in all of these areas, we believe we have failed in some way, that we don't quite fit the bill.

The problem is not only that we want all of the above, but also that we believe that this is in fact possible as well. The media constantly feeds us with images of winners: people who are extremely successful and rich and possess a perfect smile and a flat stomach. And we don't even need to feast our eyes on celebrities to see this. A mere 15 minutes on Facebook, Instagram or LinkedIn is usually enough to leave you thinking that everyone is happy and successful and leads an incredibly interesting life. Everyone except you, that is. The more perfect other people's lives seem to us, the more likely we are to regard our own lives as incomplete. We only ever see the exterior of other people's lives, but we are all too aware of our own deficiencies under the surface. And that is why we often feel inferior to others.

Fortunately, the market has provided us with the perfect solution: you can rid yourself of that feeling of inferiority by spending money. We are told that we can consume our way to happiness and recognition. Just purchase product X and fortune will smile on you again – at least that's what we're told. Buying stuff is the way to solve your problems and enrich your life.

No surprise, therefore, that we often get stuck on the 'hedonic treadmill'. We spend much of our time consuming things in the hope that they will make us happy. Things that mislead us with their promise of happiness. In reality, however, the things we consume rarely make us happy, beyond the first moment or two. The 'buyer's high' soon wears off and we find ourselves right back where we started. When you buy that shiny new laptop, for the first few days you will be delighted each time you turn it on. But the feeling will wear off after only a week or so. And when that happens, when that brief period of pleasure has passed, all we can do is try to find the same sensation again by purchasing another product. Like the metaphorical hamster on the treadmill, we end up chasing product after product in the hope that this will somehow enrich our lives.

It's not just our pursuit of stuff that keeps us on the treadmill. We also consume experiences in a similar fashion. Experiences – everything from weddings and holidays to parties and festivals – have also become a kind of product to be consumed at our leisure. The idea is that everything is there to be experienced and we *should* experience everything so that we don't miss out on anything or feel excluded. This is why we fill not only our work but also our free time with activities, such as sports and social events. We are so aware of the large number of interesting activities on offer that we are afraid of missing out on even a single one. People suffer severely nowadays from FOMO: the Fear Of Missing Out. And worse still, we often arrive at one of our scheduled events only to find ourselves wondering if maybe something even more fun is going on somewhere else?

Our solution is to try to fit everything in or at least to plan our lives so efficiently that we can get the maximum return from our time. If I cycle over to my friend Dick's place for an hour directly after my yoga class finishes at nine, on my way back I will be able drop in to see Sophie and wish her a happy birthday and still have time to squeeze in an episode of *Succession* before hitting the hay.

It sounds perfectly doable – you get to cross everything off your list and you don't miss out on anything – but it is not necessarily the best strategy. All that planning takes a lot of brainpower and means you are always in a rush. In fact, you end up watching the clock half of the time. After your yoga class you become annoyed when you have to wait your turn to shower – 'I'm in a hurry for Chrissakes!' At Dick's you keep checking your phone so that you won't be late for Sophie's party. At the party you keep your jacket on because you won't be staying long. And when you finally flop onto the couch at home, you fall asleep before the opening scene in *Succession* has even started.

Organising your evening in the manner described above would probably mean that you spend so long trying to schedule it properly you forget to relax, which was the point in the first place. The risk is that you become so occupied with planning how to get to your next port of call on time that you forget to *be* where you actually *are* at the moment. In fact, your haste will more than likely spoil each of your activities that evening. Because of our urge to fit everything in, we often miss out on the very things we want to experience. It may sound very appealing to have a diary crammed with things to do, but it almost never produces the desired result. Your free time is meant for relaxation and recovery, and that is impossible when you have too much on your plate. Doing everything all at once is a recipe for stress. You need to make clear choices and allow for a bit of wriggle room. What deserves your attention and when? Maybe you could go see Dick on Tuesday instead so that you have more time for a proper chat. Forget the party, you'll see Sophie next week anyway and she won't mind. You could fit in an episode of *Succession* after yoga on Thursday, but only if you're not feeling too tired. No matter how much we may fear it, missing out on some things is basically inevitable.

## Overclocking

In computers that were built 15 or more years ago it was possible to speed up the processor by changing the clock rate. This made the computer system think that time was passing quicker than it actually was. This practice is known as 'over-clocking' and it was used to make a computer work a lot faster than it was originally designed to. The results were usu-ally fantastic – you got a lot more processing power with the same hardware – but it shortened the lifespan of your com-puter considerably. You also had to provide the computer with extra cooling to prevent the processor from burning out.

Today, in a similar fashion, we try to outsmart our own clock by squeezing as much out of our time as possible. We work hard. We play even harder. And then we try extra hard to relax and detox. We try ten different ways of losing weight, quickly. Instead of taking the time to tell a well-spun story, we prepare elevator pitches.[3] Top chef Jamie Oliver recently launched a new instalment of his popular '30-minute meals' series, this time called '15-minute meals', as if taking 30 minutes to pre-pare a meal is beyond us these days. We resort to time man-agement so that we can do more work in less time. For example, we fill the time we 'lose' while travelling with work we can do on the fly. We are becoming more and more like the characters in our favourite TV series – always bursting with energy, always busy doing important things and permanently 'switched on'. You certainly never see them sprawled out on the couch at home.

It can all be done faster, better, more efficiently, and so we always feel like we are never quite good enough, never employing our 'full potential' and not making every second count. However, the race against time is one we can never win. The clock will tick on relentlessly no matter how hard you try to catch it out. Time is something you can only spend once. When it's gone it cannot be retrieved. In the words of the author Seth Godin, 'You can't save up time. You can't refuse to spend it. You can't set it aside. Either you're spending your time, or your time is spending you.'

Our time on Earth is finite. Depending on how long you live, you only have a certain number of hours to use up. If you reach the age of 88, you will have lived a total of 750,000 hours. Given that you are reading this book, the first 20 years of your life – a total of 175,000 hours – are probably already behind you. A long career spanning 48 years during which you worked eight hours a day, excluding weekends, adds up to 100,000 hours of working time. Assuming that you spend half of your time on 'maintenance' (sleeping, eating, exercise, on the toilet, doing the shopping, commuting) this means you have approximately 100,000 hours left over for everything else: time with your family, friends and loved ones, reading books, visiting places you want to see and doing the things you want to do. In other words, the time you can devote to others, to your own development and to the things that make life worth living. And from that total you would have to subtract the two hours (or five years and four months of your life) that statistics say you spend on average each day on social media.

You could also draw up a budget for your time. Of course, this doesn't mean you need to be Scrooge-like with your time, but you should have some kind of a plan for how you want to spend your waking hours. The only way to create time for the things you want to do is to omit other things that are less important.

There are 168 hours in a week. Let's assume you spend 56 of those hours sleeping and 32 on daily activities like cooking, eating, washing and cleaning. If you have a full-time job, you work 40 hours a week. This means you have 38 hours left over for all the other stuff you do: time for family and friends, quality time with your partner, exercise, hobbies, reading, shopping, DIY, meditating, playing music, etc. This also includes, of course, the hours you spend on Instagram, Facebook, WhatsApp, Snapchat and Netflix.

**Division of hours per week**

- sleep
- maintenance
- work
- everything else

Draw up a time budget. How do you spend the hours in a full week? It might help to imagine that your time is worth €250 per hour. Would that change the way you look at how you spend your time? What would you most like to spend your time on, given how precious that resource is? How can you 'invest' your time wisely? And what is not 'worth' your time?

There is a limited number of hours you can spend each week on the things you find important, pleasant or interesting. Trying to cram too much into that period of time (and not doing anything fully as a result) – or focusing only on what you 'should' or 'have to' do – is a surefire way of wasting your precious time. It is better to do fewer things to the full than lots of things by half.

## Choice overload

Ever since I subscribed to Netflix I have been experiencing the same problem over and over again. When I finish watching a particular series I immediately embark on an endless search for what I want to watch next. I spend 15 minutes scrolling enthusiastically through all the different series on offer. I select a few for my own list and then choose one to watch. However, I usually end up switching the new series off after only a few minutes of the first episode. After all my searching and optimising, this one should have been absolutely perfect, but that rarely proves to be the case. So I try a different series, and then another and another, until I think to myself: to hell with that! Tired of searching through the countless options, I eventually decide to watch an episode of *House, MD* that I have seen millions of times before – one I know I will enjoy.

We make hundreds of choices every day – from the relatively trivial (Will I have toast or fruit for breakfast? Which series will I watch tonight?) to the hugely important (Do I want to move house? Should I look for another job? Would I be happier in a different relationship?) and everything in between.

If you're not careful, the pressure to choose can easily become a source of stress. There is even a term for this phenomenon: choice overload.

Choice overload is caused by what psychologist Barry Schwartz calls 'the paradox of choice'. This refers to our belief that having many options to choose from is essentially a good thing. If you have thousands of options, you can always choose the one that is best for you. This will have the maximum effect on your sense of happiness and well-being, or at least that's what we believe. According to Schwartz, however, it doesn't work like this in reality. Within this the-more-options-the-better framework we often overlook one important factor: the amount of time and energy you have to spend on making all those choices. The more options there are, the longer it takes you to choose and the more difficult the choice becomes. And when there are too many options it can lead to more stress, poor choices and even a tendency not to choose at all.

The weighing of options when making a choice can be very strenuous for your brain. It's not so difficult when you have to choose between white bread and brown. But when the options also include wholemeal, corn, sunflower seeds, spelt, farmhouse, fibre-rich, gluten-free, low-salt, thick-cut and finely-sliced – all at different price points and with different pros and cons – the choice becomes exponentially more complicated. Not only do you have to compare the different options, but you also have to figure out the relevant criteria on which to base your choice. Is your choice based on flavour, price or health considerations? Have you managed to choose from the myriad of options available? If so, then well done!

Here's your loaf of bread, now you only have 99 more decisions to make today.

It is possible to spend a large portion of your day simply trying to make the right choices. Let's say you're looking for a new pair of trousers. There are hundreds of options to choose from: slim fit, regular fit, stone-washed, boot cut, and in all kinds of colours. You can even have them tailor-made to suit your own personal tastes. However, the question quickly arises whether it is worth all the time you have to spend on sifting through the various options. There is little evidence that being able to choose a pair of trousers that perfectly matches all our preferences actually makes us any happier.

People differ greatly in the strategies they use to make choices. So-called 'maximisers' try to pick the best possible option by carefully comparing all of the available options with each other, weighing up the pros and cons and establishing precisely what they need. When making a choice, maximisers try to answer the question: is this definitely the best option? Taking everything into consideration, is this the best pair of trousers I can buy? This is an extremely effective method – you always end up choosing the ideal option – but it is by no means the most efficient one. Maximisers are the kind of people you see walking around town looking for the restaurant that offers the best price/quality ratio and which is, of course, always around the next corner, or the next. By the time the maximiser has finally chosen a restaurant, they are usually tired and grumpy as a result of their dramatically depleted blood sugar level.

At the other end of the spectrum is the satisficer: the champion of fast decision-making. The satisficer uses a number of specific criteria to quickly choose an option they believe will fit the bill. They ask: Is this option good enough? Does this pair of trousers match my criteria? This strategy almost never results in the ideal choice – primarily because not all of the options have been considered – but in a choice that the satisficer is happy to accept. Satisficing has one major advantage: you arrive at a decision much quicker because you don't try to weigh up all the options. And the choice you make is usually 'good enough'.

Research has shown that maximisers tend not to be as happy, optimistic and satisfied as satisficers, are more prone to depression and perfectionism and regret their choices more often.[4] There is a logical explanation for this. If the question is: 'Is this the best possible choice?' disappointment is always baked into the strategy.

> Keep a daily record of the decisions you make and how you arrived at them. For which choices do you employ the maximiser strategy? For which choices are you a satisficer? Are you happy with the amount of time you spend making choices? Which decisions take up too much of your time?

The solution for the problem of choice overload does not involve deciding to employ a satisficer strategy on a constant basis. Some choices (where you wish to work, what you want to study, deciding on a financial strategy) are simply too big and too important. In such cases the best option is to examine all of the available options thoroughly and to compare them with each other before making a final decision. However, decisions that require a maximiser strategy are few and far between. For most choices, a quick and satisfying strategy is perfectly fine. Life is full of these more or less trivial decisions. In the case of most decisions you are better off saving the brainpower and mental resources you could otherwise be spending on optimising for more important stuff.

I recently visited a restaurant where the menu was so extensive it included a table of contents. Just reading all the various options would have taken me nearly half an hour. So instead I just picked a page at random and chose a dish that sounded okay, which took me no more than two minutes. Knowing when you need to make a perfect and deliberate choice and when a quick 'okay' choice will do can spare you a lot of stress. You also need to consider how much of your precious time you are willing to spend on making a decision. Don't be afraid to go for speed when making less important decisions instead of trying to find the Ultimate Option.

With all the digital documentation, reviews and price comparison sites at our disposal, it is easy to get lost in the maze of options when making a choice. There is always more information to be found somewhere. If you fancy a weekend away in Paris, you can choose from 1,445 different accommodations options on Booking.com, all with their own perks and drawbacks. You could easily spend half a day comparing all the possibilities. That is why it is sometimes useful to set a time limit for your choice, based on how important the decision is to you: I want to spend no more than two hours on booking my weekend; when the alarm goes off I will pick the best option I have found. It doesn't really bother me what kind of cutlery I buy, so I want to have made my mind up within 30 minutes. The Perfect Choice – if such a thing even exists – is almost never worth the amount of time it demands.

# The dictator in your pocket

Imagine a man being transported in a time machine from the 1950s to the present day and being dropped in the middle of New York City. Walking around goggle-eyed in his suit and hat, what would strike him most about his new surroundings? Perhaps the mass of advertisement hoardings and screens with their never-ending stream of information. Or maybe the sound made by the cars – or perhaps the lack of it compared with the automobiles back in his time. More likely, however, is that our man from the Fifties would be most surprised by the mobile telephones that everyone spends their time staring at. I imagine he'd write something like this in his diary: 'Modern day humans carry a square black device around in their pockets connected to a set of earphones. It is obviously their most valuable possession, given the amount of time they spend looking at it.'

Imagine then proudly telling this curious time traveller about this wonder of technology we call a mobile phone. 'It's so handy. You can contact anyone you like anywhere in the world, and whenever you like, too, and you can immediately see if someone is calling you or has sent you a message!', you might explain excitedly. Our time traveller could be forgiven for taking a moment to think before replying: 'But why would you want any of that?'

We use that small, shiny supercomputer in our pocket for almost everything. It is our shopping list, our means of contacting the outside world, our step counter, our source of amusement, our route planner, our alarm clock, our news channel, our soundtrack and a whole lot more. However, this little device also has a darker side. It often behaves like a mini dictator. It demands our attention at the drop of a hat. Ping! An e-mail! Ping! A message from your friend, Rob! Ping! You have been invited to play Farm House! Ping! A new potential match! Please update your settings! Ping! Ping! Now, please!!

We have become quite addicted to these smart little devices. According to a recent trend survey, we check our phone an average of 150 times each day. In 2017 adults spent an average of three hours a day on their phone. And remember, these are average figures. They include my grandmother, who pays her mobile phone no more than a few minutes' attention each day. It will come as no surprise, therefore, that the figures for young adults (18–24 years old) are much higher, even as high as eight to ten hours a day according to some estimates. While writing this book I decided to track my own screen time using the Screentime app. With a screen time of one hour and 40 minutes per day I was well below the average, which is probably not unusual for someone who is busy writing a book about stress. Nevertheless, the app revealed that I spend 11% of my waking hours staring at a small screen and that I check my smartphone a shocking 46 times each day.

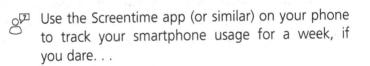 Use the Screentime app (or similar) on your phone to track your smartphone usage for a week, if you dare. . .

We use our smartphone for literally everything these days. Whenever we feel ourselves becoming bored, we reach for the device in the pursuit of distraction. If you walk down a busy street and look around you, you may feel a little unnerved by what you see: more than half the people are likely to be staring at their phone, making a call using earphones or otherwise wired up to the Matrix. It's as if we have fallen in love with that little device. We stare into its eyes more often than we do our loved one's (since the arrival of mobile phones people actually look at each other a lot less than they used to, which is really rather saddening). For the majority of people, the screen on their smartphone is often the first thing they see when they wake up in the morning and the last thing they see before they fall asleep at night. Doctors are now beginning to express concerns about how smartphones are affecting our posture: our habit of looking down at our phone is leading to significantly more neck complaints.

The real test of a possible addiction is: can you do without? In an experiment at a university in the United States, students were randomly divided into two groups: a telephone-free group and a telephone-on-silent group. In the first group the students were asked to hand over their phones to the researchers. The students in the second group were allowed to keep their phones, as long as they were switched to silent mode and stored in a bag. They were then asked not to check their telephone for the duration of the experiment. They were also asked to fill in a questionnaire about their level of anxiety every 20 minutes. The results showed that in both groups the average-to-zealous phone users became more anxious as the experiment went on. This effect was significantly greater in the telephone-free group compared with the telephone-on-silent group – the more distance between our device and us, the more anxious we become. In other words, we react so adversely to being separated from our phone that it often sends us into a state of panic.

There are other reasons, too, why we are so addicted to our mobile devices. Studies have shown that our brain gives us a tiny shot of dopamine each time we receive a notification.

This results in a little moment of happiness each time we reach for our phone, which explains why we are so attached to the thing. We pay more attention to our next fix of smartphone dopamine than we do to our next meal, our sleeping habits and our relationships with others. No wonder the most recent hype in travel is a mobile phone detox at a luxury resort, where you have to hand over your phone upon arrival before participating in group discussions about your withdrawal symptoms.

Naturally, we have an excellent excuse for our mobile phone addiction: our modern way of living demands that we have one. We simply can't do without. Our phone has become an intrinsic part of the way in which we experience the world around us – a kind of extension of our physical selves. It keeps us up to date with the latest news, allows us to react quickly to situations and helps us to organise our lives. And as with all addictions, we tend to play down the negatives: it really isn't such a bad thing, and anyway everyone is doing it! But this is far from the truth. Our mobile phone is probably the greatest single cause of stress in our lives, apart from our work. Facebook, WhatsApp, Instagram and Tinder have us all tightly in their grip with their push notifications and this is beginning to have dire consequences for our health. Our intense focus on our phones is seriously affecting our ability to concentrate.

Our mobile devices also have a negative impact on our social lives. In fact, research suggests that just having a phone in plain view on the table in front of you affects the quality of the conversation you are conducting with someone. The phone doesn't even need to be 'doing' anything. But when it becomes active with ringtones and pings our phone makes us even more restless and increases our stress levels: 'Hey you, pay me some attention, NOW!' As such, it invades every other activity we engage in; we use our phones when we're out for a walk, whenever we're waiting and even while driving. My mother got it wrong: staring at a screen all the time does not give you square eyes. What it does give you, however, is a permanent sense of restlessness.

The idea that we need to be online at all times means we can be interrupted by our phone at any moment. This may not happen all the time, of course, but the possibility is always there. The spectre of technology is lurking around every corner.

In his book *Present Shock* the media theorist Douglas Rushkoff provides the following example. Imagine you have taken your children to the park for the day. Your telephone rings and you see that it is your neighbour calling. You have come to the park to spend some quality time with your kids, so you decide not to take the call – whatever it is, it can probably wait. However, while you are walking around the park with your children you find yourself wondering: Why did the neighbour call? Is there something up? Despite the fact that you decided not to take the call, your free time with the kids has been interrupted anyway.

It is not all doom and gloom, however. There is also some good news: it is relatively easy to protect yourself from the negative effects of your mobile phone addiction. It does require some willpower, however. It involves jumping in at the deep end and accepting that less interruption means being less contactable too. And that is never an easy thing, as we saw in the study with the students.

If you want to have less stress in your life, there is no need to trade your smartphone in for an old Nokia that only requires recharging once a week (although I know enough people who swear by their 3310). What you do need to do, however, is change your idea of how available you are to others: it is you and not your mobile phone that should dictate how and when you may be contacted. You can turn off the push notifications in your settings, for example. This will prevent you from being distracted by the persistent pinging in your pocket. You will still have access to all the information you need, but then at a time of your own choosing, not when someone decides to distract you. Tell your friends you consider the good old phone call your urgent medium and that answering any other kind of message may take a little bit more time. Leave those WhatsApp groups that take up too much of your attention; don't worry, you're absolutely allowed to! Or follow the example of author Timothy Ferriss, who turns his phone to flight mode every evening and only switches it back on after he has completed all his important tasks the following morning.

> What things could you change in order to combat the effects of technostress? What steps can you take to become less dependent on your phone and social media? And what can you do to be less of a disrupting factor in other people's lives, too?

## Organising stuff

The following may sound familiar: it is the weekend and I decide not to open my mailbox. This is my time off, after all, and I'm made of tough stuff, so I'm sure I'll manage. I stick to my decision for the rest of the morning until, around lunchtime, I find myself becoming restless and eventually give in to the temptation to take a peek at my inbox. It turns out that I have received an e-mail that requires my attention but is not extremely urgent. I decide to wait until Monday morning before sending a reply. However, after I have closed my laptop and returned to cleaning the coffee machine (or some other typical weekend job, such as arranging the jars of herbs in the kitchen in alphabetical order), I realise that the bloody e-mail is stuck in my head. I even find myself literally formulating my reply in my mind.

This is an example of what is known as a 'cognitive loop', a thought that continues to occupy your mind until you take the required action. Once it starts, a loop will not stop until a solution to the problem has been found. It will remain in the back of your mind and continue to remind you of the need to do something about it. Whenever you let your thoughts run free, your mind becomes filled with these kinds of open loops. Even if you are busy doing something else, they won't stop until you do what they demand of you.

Have you ever found yourself wondering whether you turned the gas off after dinner or remembered to lock the front door after going out? Then you know how tenacious these loops can be. They won't let go until you have responded in an adequate manner and in the meantime it is almost impossible to concentrate on anything else.

We deal with cognitive loops on a daily basis. A loop can be opened by an unexpected bill that needs paying or a mental note to yourself not to forget to buy eggs when you go to the supermarket. The unread e-mails in your inbox are all potential loops, too, as is every text message you receive, every idea that crosses your mind and every job around the house that needs doing.

Walking around with a head full of cognitive loops is like having 50 tabs open simultaneously in your internet browser. Your computer's memory becomes saturated and everything starts slowing down before eventually crashing. You can get away with having a handful of loops open at any given moment. But if you have 20 of them demanding your attention all at the same time, you will inevitably end up feeling like you are constantly playing catch-up.

You can reduce the amount of stress in your life dramatically by reducing the number of loops that are active in your head at any given time. One way of achieving this is to minimise the number of external distractions when you are focusing on a particular task. Switching your phone to flight mode, not opening your e-mail and telling your colleagues when they may disturb you and when not reduces the risk of your concentration being broken by an unexpected loop. It also helps to write things down whenever they pop into your head so that you don't have to go to the trouble of remembering them. Whenever such a loop opens (for example, when you suddenly remember you need to cancel your subscription to some service or other), make sure to jot it down in a notebook or send it to yourself in an e-mail that you can read later. This will stop that annoying voice in your head from continually asking, 'Did I already cancel my subscription or not?' It is much easier to forget about a loop after you have written it down, as you know it will pop up again at a more suitable moment.

When you have managed to get a loop under control by filing it away to be read later, the next step is to convert your note into an actionable task on your to-do list. To close a loop as quickly as possible, simply ask yourself this question: how can I solve this particular problem with the least amount of trouble? An excellent tool for this is the two-minute rule developed by time management guru, David Allen: if something takes two minutes or less to do, the best thing is to do it straight away. All other tasks should be scheduled for when you have enough time to tackle them. It is much easier to close a loop when you are sure you can complete a task later on.

> Draw up a list of the 'open ends' that are currently on your mind. Identify what you need to do to close each of these loops as quickly as possible. Perhaps by tackling a loop immediately or finding a way of reminding yourself of the loop later on so that you can let it go for now.

## Tackling the symptoms

There's no shortage of commercial solutions you can use to create more calm in your life. The rising popularity of remedies that help us to relax more shows us just how busy our lives have become. You can go on a detox weekend to combat stress or sign up for one of the countless yoga classes or mindfulness courses on offer. At your local supermarket you can choose between five different kinds of herbal 'calming' tea, and add one of the multitude of healthy living magazines to your shopping trolley while you're at it. Or, when all else fails, you can buy yourself an adult colouring book (yes, these exist!).

Unfortunately, creating peace and calm in your head requires a lot more than making yourself a cup of herbal tea and sitting down for an hour to colour in a few pictures (though this does no harm, of course). Neither does a detox weekend offer a long-term solution, as it usually amounts to little more than tackling the symptoms and does nothing about the causes. To find a genuine sense of calm you need to go a lot further and deal with things like managing your time more efficiently and making clear choices about where (and where not) to focus your attention. And it would do us no harm at all to substitute our FOMO more often for our FOBO: Fear Of Burning Out.

---

You can reduce your daily stress levels by:

- letting go of the idea that you ought to experience as much as you can all of the time;
- making clear choices about what is worth your time and what is not;
- thinking long and hard about which choices are worth devoting a lot of your time to;
- paying less attention to the dictator in your pocket;
- minimising the number of things in your head that have to be organised, as they can quickly eat up all of your energy.

---

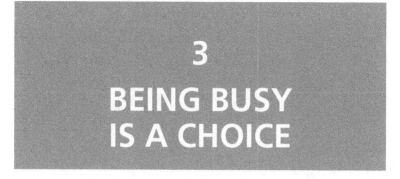

3
# BEING BUSY IS A CHOICE

Being busy is a choice; probably not the kind of thing you want to hear right now. It may even raise the hairs on the back of your neck. What?! Is this arrogant psychologist seriously trying to tell me that it was my own choice to lead such a busy life?! Well, yes and no. No one is ever going to offer you a lifetime subscription to stress and pressure. It's much more complicated than that. But you are the one who decides how you want to live your life. You get to decide how much stress you are prepared to tolerate. So yes, when you lead a busy life it is essentially your own choice.

Of course, being busy is not necessarily always a bad thing. In fact, there are plenty of reasons why you might actually want to be busy: to further your career; because you want to learn more; because you want to raise your children well; because you want to make a difference in the world. Or a combination of all these things. Sometimes you have to sacrifice your peace of mind to do what you have to do.

Your busy life may also be the result of your own character or habits. Expecting perfect results, for example, or thinking that others expect perfection from you. It could be that the expectations you have of yourself are a source of stress. Or the feeling that you are responsible for things that may not be your responsibility at all: 'I'll look after organising the family holiday because otherwise it will never happen!' Perhaps you find it difficult to say 'no' to people because you don't want them to think badly of you – a quality others often use against us. Or when you think, rightfully or not, that you are essentially indispensable at work or in other areas of your life because no one else can take your place – also a very good way of becoming stressed. You might even believe that you have no choice in the matter, that you are simply at the mercy of other people's expectations.

This chapter discusses a number of very human qualities that most of us can identify with. These qualities are often related to the way we were brought up or how we were taught to deal with problems. They are not 'flaws' in our character as such, but they certainly do trip us up on a regular basis.

You can tackle the sources of stress we identified in the previous chapters by living your life differently. However, there are also sources of stress you can eliminate by *thinking differently*. Too many people believe they are condemned to living a stressful life and feel completely powerless to do anything about it. But we are almost never entirely powerless. Everyone can choose to lead a more relaxed and less stressful life – that's my own personal conviction. However, you first have to realise that you do, in fact, have a choice.

## *Have to* versus *want to*

Some of the students I teach share a common trait. When they pass one of their exams they are usually very proud of themselves for having studied so hard and not succumbing to the pressure during the exam (and rightly so!). They are delighted with their grade and believe they should be amply rewarded for their efforts. It's a very different story, however, when they fail an exam. Then they tend to blame everything and anyone but themselves. The questions were too difficult or covered topics they hadn't been taught. They had to take the exam at a ridiculous time ('Who on earth is awake and alert at nine o'clock in the morning?!'). The exam supervisors were making too much noise and their lecturer's terrible accent meant they hadn't understood a word of what they were supposed to learn in the first place. It's clear to them that their poor results are the fault of everyone else and certainly not their own. They appear to overlook the possibility that their disappointing grades may have something to do with the fact that they spent the evening before swilling beer in the pub until closing time.

Blaming everyone but ourselves is often our way of dealing with things that are unpleasant but also unavoidable. Laying the blame at the feet of others or pointing the finger at Lady Fortune is our way of diverting attention away from ourselves. If your misery is all someone else's fault, you don't have to face the possibility that you may in fact be (at least partly) at fault yourself. It allows you to deal with the disappointment without having to take a long, hard look at yourself in the mirror. This applies not only to poor grades but also to how we react to things like getting fired, breaking up or making a bad investment. And, of course, how we react to stress.

People differ in the extent to which they feel they are in charge of their own life. Those with an *internal attribution style* believe they control their life themselves. They view the events in their life – both positive and negative – as the result of their own actions. People with an *external attribution style*, on the other hand, tend to consistently assign control over their life to factors outside of themselves, particularly with regard to the negative aspects. Some external factor appears to control their behaviour or destiny: 'I had no choice' or 'That's just the way it is'. External attribution is akin to taking on the role of the victim: 'I am who I am and I do what I do because that is what others expect of me or because I'm forced to behave this way. I can't do anything about that.'

Studies have shown that an external attribution style corresponds with a higher level of stress, a lower degree of life and career success and feelings of helplessness, depression and anxiety. People with an internal attribution style tend to have more confidence, fewer negative emotions and more success. In my classes, it is typically those students who recognise their own role in failing to achieve good grades – and are prepared to change their behaviour the next time around – who manage to improve their score at the next exam. Conversely, the students who refuse to believe that they play a role in their own failure inevitably end up making the same mistakes again and again.

You can often tell whether a person has an internal or external style of attribution from the kind of language they use. People with an external attribution style tend to use the phrase 'have to' more frequently, while those with an internal attribution style are more likely to use the words 'want to'. When you feel you 'have to' do something you are a prisoner of your own circumstances or the will of those around you. Something or someone is forcing you to act in a particular way. On the other hand, if you 'want to' do something, you claim the responsibility for yourself and it gives you the feeling that you are in control of what happens in your life. When you keep telling yourself 'I have to go to work today' you put the power to choose in other people's hands. Saying to yourself 'I want to go to work today' means that the choice is yours (even if you don't really feel like going). The end result is the same, of course, but there is a big difference in terms of how you feel about it. You could also choose *not* to go to work today but then decide to go anyway, for reasons that are important to you. The outcome may be the same but the difference is that it involves a considered choice instead of an obligation.

There is one golden rule if you want to change your style of attribution from an external one to a more internal one: fake it till you make it. You need to keep asking yourself the question: how would I behave if I was in control of the situation? What would I do differently? Another strategy is to change the kind of language you use, as described below.

Try to avoid using the phrase 'I have to' for a whole day. If you feel the urge to say those words, ask yourself: who is telling me I 'have to'? Do I have a choice in the matter, and if so, what are my options? Then try rephrasing what you want to say by substituting 'I have to' for phrases like 'I can', 'I want to' or 'I choose to'.

A person's style of attribution is rarely ever exclusively internal or external. Most of us have a mix of the two, with a tendency towards one or the other depending on the situation.

No matter how good you are at retaining mental control of your own life, there are some things that are heavily dependent on external factors.

For example, you usually have some control over how a job interview will proceed. But whether you are offered the position or not depends also upon the quality of the other candidates and the kind of person the interview panel is looking for. However, there is a psychological advantage attached to having an internal style of attribution. If you are in the habit of allowing external factors to have the upper hand ('I can't do anything about the situation') you are more likely to suffer from stress: if you don't make your own choices, someone else will do it for you.

It's not always easy taking responsibility for your own actions – for example, when you have to admit that you haven't handled a particular matter very well – but doing so on a regular basis will boost your self-confidence and your capacity to deal with stress, simply because you have decided to take control of your own life.

Being Busy is a Choice

## Being busy versus being under pressure

If you feel under pressure, it's because you are very busy. Right? Well, not quite.

'Being busy' has to do with your workload, the actual amount of work you have to do: the number of hours you work each week, the number of tasks you have to complete in a day, the amount of time you spend in meetings, etc. Your workload is something you can measure objectively. Being busy can be expressed in numbers: the number of minutes spent on a task, the number of pages you have to write, the number of targets you reach (or don't) and the kind of 'work' you have to do in your free time as well – appointments, jobs around the house and managing your affairs.

'Being under pressure', on the other hand, has more to do with how you experience your workload at the subjective level. This can include the amount of responsibility you feel towards your work or your team and the pressure that comes with trying to meet a deadline. How do you react when you are subject to time constraints? When something goes wrong do you panic or are you able to remain calm? The amount of enjoyment and the sense of meaning you take from your work also plays an important role in how you react to pressure: the more satisfaction you get from your work, the better you are able to stand the heat.

You would expect there to be a direct link between being busy and being under pressure. After all, you don't feel under

61

pressure when your workload is light, but the busier you become the more pressure you feel. Sounds pretty logical. Visually it would look something like this:

Workload →

However, it doesn't seem to work like this at all. The amount of pressure you feel doesn't necessarily correlate with how busy you are. In fact, some people feel constantly under pressure regardless of how busy they are. These people feel stressed even when their workload appears to be manageable. They feel under pressure not only when they are busy but also when they are not. Their chart would look something like this:

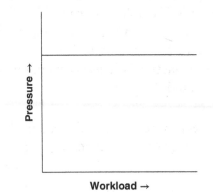

Workload →

The reverse is also possible: that you never feel under pressure, regardless of how heavy your workload is. These people have the capacity to remain calm under pressure and to keep a cool head even under the most trying circumstances. They don't get rattled when they are very busy and so their chart looks like this:

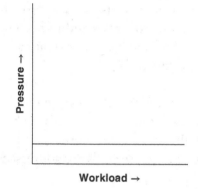

Apparently there is another category of people who feel less pressure as their workload increases, but I've yet to meet someone who fits that description.

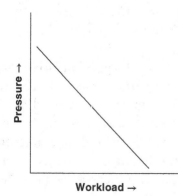

So, there's a difference between being under pressure and being busy. Both can be managed effectively, of course, but the approach is different for each one. If you are the type of person whose challenges in terms of stress are related primarily to being under pressure, you will find the answers you require at the psychological end of the scale (for example, in the information provided in this chapter). The most important thing for you in this case would probably be to learn how to recognise signs of stress and to become familiar with at least a couple of techniques that you can use to combat acute stress (see Chapter 6).

If, on the other hand, the challenges you face are more closely related to being busy, and consequently to how you manage your time, then the answer lies more in the areas of planning and setting priorities (these skills are addressed in Chapter 7).

## Procrastination

Psychologists have long been perplexed by our capacity to postpone important tasks. Why is it that we often leave things that we need to do until the very last minute, even when we are motivated enough to do them?

In a popular TED talk, blogger Tim Urban explains his own tendency to procrastinate. In the talk Tim reveals that his thoughts and actions are usually steered by two characters: the Rational Decision-Maker and the Instant Gratification Monkey. The Rational Decision-Maker likes for Tim to focus his attention on the important stuff in life as efficiently as possible. The Instant Gratification Monkey has other things in mind, however, like doing stuff that is enjoyable and amusing in the short term, such as playing with the cat or scrolling through Reddit. When, at the prompting of the Rational Decision-Maker, Tim decides to do something useful it doesn't take long for the Monkey to butt in, mainly because he has no intention of allowing Tim to postpone the fun stuff. These two characters then get into a struggle with each other for control of the wheel, while Tim fails to get anything done in the meantime.

The impasse is only broken when, just before the deadline, a third character appears on the scene: the Panic Monster, a somewhat hysterical type who always insists that the important stuff gets done NOW. The Panic Monster knows how to send the Instant Gratification Monkey packing and get Tim down to work, albeit not quite in the most relaxed or pleasant manner imaginable.

What things are you currently putting on the long finger? These can include major things like applying for a new job or small things, such as cleaning your kitchen. Why do you keep putting them off? Make a list and we will return to it later on.

The psychology of procrastination works as follows. We humans almost invariably want not one but multiple things at the same time. We can have different motivations at the same moment in time, too. It often happens that the things we desire are at loggerheads with each other – for instance when we want a responsible and meaningful job but also want lots of free time for relaxing as well.

To make it even more difficult we can both want and not want something at the same time, which often results in inner conflict. Imagine you have decided to ask your boss for a raise. You believe you have good reasons for doing so and that it's worth your while bringing it up. At the same time you want to maintain a good relationship with your boss. You are wary of coming across as too aggressive and cause them to dislike you as a result. In the end you decide to shelve the matter and save the e-mail you have written to your boss about your salary for another day.

Procrastinating behaviour is often evasive behaviour: by postponing something we try to avoid facing an unpleasant situation for as long as possible. The things we try to avoid are often the things we find important but also very difficult. The difficulty can lie in your belief that you are bound to fail at the thing you continue to postpone – it will suddenly and surely become obvious that you are just not up to the task. Or you would simply prefer to avoid the effort required to see it through. For instance, you would like to learn Spanish because you will soon be taking a trip to Chile, but you are put off by the amount of work potentially involved and the fear that you might not succeed – excellent reasons for postponing your decision until the last possible moment.

It often happens that you have to do something difficult now in order to attain some desirable but very distant goal in the future: studying hard to get a good grade, biting the bullet and discussing that pay rise with your boss, writing regularly and diligently in the hope that you will someday manage to finish your book. It is often far easier and more rewarding to do something that is more enjoyable and fun in the short term – binge-watching a series on Netflix, for instance (and more often than not we are prepared to tolerate the guilty feeling that comes with succumbing to the temptation).

And then there's the fact that it is very easy to assign all these difficult tasks to your 'future self' so that your present self doesn't have to deal with them. Unfortunately, this usually involves us grossly overestimating the capabilities of our future self: 'I don't feel like doing it now, but tomorrow I'm going to get everything on that list done!' After all, we imagine our future self as always being in the best of moods and bursting with energy. Everything will be fine if you just postpone the hard stuff because when tomorrow comes around you will surely be incredibly motivated and extraordinarily productive. We blatantly ignore the fact that our future self will probably want to postpone everything, too, or may just end up having a bad day. If your Present Self is anything to go by, then your Future Self will probably have some reservations about doing the hard stuff, too.

The greater the task that faces us, the greater our resistance often is to getting on with the job. That's why it can sometimes help to split a large task up into smaller, more feasible steps that are easier to achieve on their own. Imagine you are planning to organise a network meeting. You can choose to write 'set up network meeting' in your diary but that will only increase the risk of procrastination because it is such a large task in itself. In terms of motivation it is probably better to split the task up into a number of clearly defined sub-tasks ('compile guest list' and 'book meeting room', for example). Making your tasks smaller reduces the risk of you postponing everything until 'later'.

> Take a look at the list I asked you to make a short while ago. Are there things on that list that could be split up into smaller, more manageable tasks? Make a list of those smaller tasks. It helps too if you describe the action required as clearly as possible.

A second tip for combatting procrastination involves you eating a frog and is admittedly a little gruesome. Imagine someone told you that you had to eat a live frog today. How would you go about it? There are two options. You could postpone it until later and carry on doing whatever it was you were doing as if nothing had happened. However, you would then spend the rest of the day thinking about how you are going to have to eat the frog before finally swallowing the pill, so to speak. The longer you wait, the more awful the prospect becomes. Then there is the other, albeit less attractive option of eating the frog immediately, before you do anything else. This requires some discipline, of course, and is far from pleasant, but at least you get to put it all behind you. As a result, the rest of your day is a doddle. After all, it can't get any worse than being forced to eat a live frog, can it?

What applies in the case of the frog also applies to other stuff we prefer to put off until tomorrow. A good piece of advice is to tackle those things you are least looking forward to at the start of your working day and before you open your mailbox or get bogged down in the stuff that demands your attention on a daily basis. This will prevent you from thinking about the difficult tasks all day until you simply can't postpone them any longer. An additional benefit is that you get to tackle these tasks at the time of day when we tend to have the most energy and willpower: in the morning – the ideal time for dealing with important matters. And remember, you can only really enjoy Netflix after you have ditched your guilty feelings.

## Perfectionism

> Imagine if I told you that you had to scrap today's most important task from your to-do list. Under no circumstances are you allowed to carry out that task. You can't postpone it until later or find some other kind of solution. How would that make you feel? How would it affect you in a practical way?

During training programmes I often give the above assignment to trainees as homework. Most of them find this thought experiment extremely difficult. They are usually quick to raise their objections, even before they have tried to solve the problem. The very thought that they are prohibited from doing a certain thing or may fail to live up to expectations is enough to derail them. They dread the prospect of not being good enough or disappointing others. And these feelings are strong even when they only *imagine* the possibility that things could go wrong.

The amount of stress you experience in your life depends partly on the demands you place upon yourself. Expecting yourself to meet every single challenge and to do everything perfectly is a guaranteed recipe for stress. The secret to living a more relaxed life is the ability to allow yourself to make mistakes.

Perfectionism is defined as the tendency to place very high demands on your own performance. Perfectionism also often goes hand in hand with a highly critical attitude towards the performance of others. It appears that when you set the bar high for yourself you do the same for others, too.

You can draw a distinction between 'healthy' and 'unhealthy' perfectionism. 'Healthy' perfectionism allows you to produce excellent work, ensures that others can always count on you and motivates you to pay attention to the details. 'Healthy' perfectionism enables you to succeed at what you are doing. But there are also serious drawbacks attached to perfectionism. It is often accompanied by stress, anxiety and the fear of coming up short. People with 'unhealthy' perfectionistic tendencies never feel they are good enough. This can be extremely frustrating and ultimately very damaging. In the words of the journalist (and perfectionist) Amanda Ruggeri: 'When perfectionists don't succeed, they don't just feel disappointment about how they did. They feel shame about who they are.'

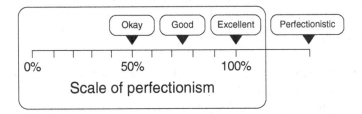

The number of perfectionists appears to have risen dramatically over the past 20 years. And that is bad news because people with perfectionistic tendencies run a much higher risk of suffering a burnout. This is not surprising, of course. If you believe that everything you do must be perfect, you will spend much more time on your work and put yourself under much more pressure. Perfectionism can also lead to a host of other problems: depression, social anxiety, eating disorders, exhaustion and sleep disorders.

Experts are now referring to perfectionism as one of the most important features of the modern era. It also has a strong cultural aspect. Over the past 30 years or so, many children in the West have been brought up with the idea that 'you can be whatever you want, as long as you work hard enough.' But if you believe that, then by definition you will also believe that you have no one to blame but yourself if you fail. This means that you and you alone are responsible for succeeding in life.

Perfectionism is often the result of an upbringing in which the level of positive attention and affection is directly related to performance. If you do well as a child at school, the compliments will flow. But when you make mistakes or do not deliver an optimal performance you will be given the cold shoulder.

The idea of perfection is deeply anchored in Western culture. We are surrounded by perfection and excellence. We revere the athletes who can run the fastest and jump the furthest. We are constantly bombarded with the most amazing success stories and our role models are famous musicians and movie stars and the head honchos at Apple and Google. In the media, perfect bodies and perfect lives are the norm. And we tell no one we had to endure a year-long diet of low-fat yoghurt and goji berries to be able to post that perfect fit girl photo on our Instagram page. We make it look easy! You could be forgiven for thinking that you are only really worth something as a human being when you perform consistently at your peak.

The reality of the situation, however, is less spectacular. You often fail to perform to the best of your ability. In fact, you rarely ever do. Our lives are full of error, whether we like it or not. It's part of being human. But we see very little of that reflected in the media or in the world around us. We simply don't see enough examples of the kinds of silly mistakes people make on a day-to-day basis to be able to readily forgive our own all-too-human faults.

When it comes to work, perfectionists never have it easy. In your job, the quality of your work is not the only important criterium you are judged by. You also score (or lose) points for the length of time it takes you to complete a task. And achieving perfection can take a long, long time. Take, for instance, the job of recording the minutes of a meeting, which are meant to be useful, easily scanned and not too time-consuming to read. If you are the kind of person who will spend forever trying to make the minutes as perfect as possible, you will quickly find yourself facing a major problem: no one wants that kind of perfection and you would be better off spending the time on something more productive.

Of particular peril to people with perfectionistic tendencies is the kind of task that you could probably spend a lot of time on but where the objective and time frame involved are far from clear. For example, your boss says to you: 'Put your ideas down in writing and we'll discuss them at a later date.' If you are a perfectionist, this kind of instruction is potentially disastrous, as you could end up working on your ideas for days on end in an effort to make them as perfect as possible. Pairing a perfectionist with a task for which there is no discernible deadline is simply asking for trouble. I have seen plenty of perfectionists working themselves silly in this kind of situation.

If you are a perfectionist and find that it is obstructing you in what you do, don't worry. Help is at hand. It is possible to tackle the 'unhealthy' aspects of your perfectionism. One essential step you must take is to increase your tolerance for making mistakes. This can be done by conducting an experiment in which you purposely allow some things to go wrong and then examine your own reaction. And because it is an experiment you won't end up paying for those mistakes. It's all in the name of science, after all.

> Allow something to go wrong on purpose once a week for the next four weeks. Start with something small the first week ('forget' to return a phone call, overlook a spelling mistake in a report) and gradually increase the size and significance of your 'mistakes'. Keep a close eye on what happens. How do the 'mistakes' make you feel? Does the feeling match your expectations? And how do the people around you react?

After you have carried out the assignment as instructed (and I presume you will, if you are a perfectionist!), you will probably realise the following: that the people around you don't have the same high expectations of your work as you do. While you might expect a perfect result every time, other people probably don't. And although you may believe you must avoid making mistakes at all costs, others are more likely to assume that you will not always operate at your peak. They have basically factored that in. For others 'good enough' is often exactly that: good enough.

In reality, there is very little that actually needs to be perfect. Naturally, some things have to be perfect, like brain surgery for example, but not many of us are required to do that kind of work. This means it is very important to create the capacity to be just 'good enough' at certain things. Try asking yourself the question: 'Is this something that needs to be perfect or is "good enough" good enough?' Opting for 'perfectly fine' instead of 'perfect' will allow you to save your perfectionism for those few moments when perfection is really required.

Perfection is often unnecessary and it costs such an awful lot of time and energy that it is rarely worth the investment. Achieving an 80% score for a task, such as writing a report, preparing for a meeting or studying for an exam, requires about 20% of your time and energy. Endeavouring to add the other 20% on top for a perfect score of 100%, however, can cost you up to 80% of your precious resources.

That last 20% (for a perfect result) is often not even worth it, if truth be told. In most cases an 80% score is more than good enough. For example, an 8 for an exam is regarded as an excellent grade. Similarly, no one will complain when the e-mail you sent them is not quite perfect but, say, 80% good – in fact, people are not even likely to notice. And more often than not your first draft of a mail or letter can usually be considered as 80% 'done'. There is often no need to write that second or third draft. We sometimes have the tendency to demand more of ourselves than the people around us actually expect of us.

Whereas your colleagues may be perfectly happy to operate at 80% of their capacity, we often feel like a failure when we do the same. Remember, for others your 80% can represent 100% of what they expect of you. An 8 is often just fine, so you can save some of your energy by trying less hard to perfect something that does not demand perfection.

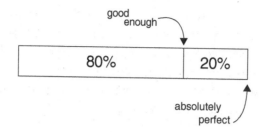

Let's look at an example. Imagine you are designing a website for your company. What would a fabulously streamlined website look like? That is your 100%. Now, what would the result that would satisfy you, the client and the user look like? What would represent a 'perfectly fine' result? That is your 80%. And if you want to be sure your work is of a high enough standard, you can aim just above that mark. This does not mean you will never have to aim for a 100% score. It's about consciously choosing the instances when you do need to aim for 100% and lowering the bar a bit for everything else.

In the coming week, select two tasks for which you will aim for an 80% score instead of 100%. First envisage the perfect outcome (A) and then the outcome that would satisfy both you and your client or manager (B). Ask yourself the question: what is good enough? The sweet spot you want to aim for lies somewhere between A and B – a little less perfect than you would like but a little more than they probably expect.

## Not my patch, sorry!

Another character trait that can cause considerable amounts of stress is a high sense of responsibility. When you feel responsible not only for your own work but that of others, too, or even for your whole team, this can lead to excessive levels of stress. People with a high sense of responsibility are 'good citizens', those without tend to enjoy life more. If you don't know what you are responsible for, you will end up feeling responsible for everything.

A few years ago I decided to go and see a career coach. I was working two jobs, which was not unusual for me at the time. I had just taken on a new position but was reluctant to let go of my old one, despite the fact that I didn't actually have enough time for both jobs. I felt obliged to hold onto my old job for fear of causing problems for others by leaving. What would they do without me? So there I stood, with one foot in one job and one foot in the other. When I told my coach about my problem she didn't hesitate to ask: 'Why are you still working there?' 'Because no one else can do my job!', I replied in all seriousness. To which she in turn replied: 'That doesn't sound plausible, and neither is it a good reason for staying.'

That was the moment I decided to quit my old job and focus fully on the new one. A misplaced sense of responsibility is never a good reason for doing anything, I figured. The fact that you are good at something does not necessarily mean that is where you should apply your talents. It is not very good for your motivation, either. I quickly realised that however competent I might consider myself to be, I am not irreplaceable.

We like to feel useful. We feel good about ourselves when we think we play an important role in a certain task: 'If I don't answer my e-mails, our customers will be mad!' or 'If I don't plan the weekend away with my friends, no one will – just wait and see!' However, this feeling of being *useful* often turns into a misguided feeling of being *irreplaceable*. You believe that the success or failure of a task is entirely dependent on your contribution. This is sometimes referred to as 'the irreplaceability illusion', with the emphasis on 'illusion'.

Imagine you broke your leg and were unable to go to work for a while. What would happen? It would certainly lead to some disruption and the person who takes over your work would probably not do it as well as you would. You would be missed. However, you would probably not be *unmissable*. That is an illusion. This knowledge can be painful for your ego but it can also be a relief. We are often haunted by guilty feelings and end up doing things because we think we are the only one who can do them. But is that really the case? If you are completely honest about it, are you really as irreplaceable as you think you are? Probably not, and that's a good thing.

At the start of this chapter we saw how stressful it can be when you believe you are not in control of your own life. On the other hand, wanting too much control can lead to problems, too. For example, when others don't do what you expect them to do. And you may end up leaving the door wide open for *social loafers*: people who, in a situation where shared responsibility is required, leave most of the work to those with a high sense of responsibility. When a group of people are working together, social loafers often try to hitch a free ride by reacting only when necessary and copping out whenever they can. Obviously, this can only happen when there is someone in the group who is prepared to assume responsibility for the end result, no matter what. This situation can be fine for everyone; everyone, that is, except the very conscientious person prepared to shoulder all the responsibility. If that happens to be you, you're out of luck. Most of the work will eventually end up on your desk. Unfortunately, some people are prone to taking advantage of another person's high sense of responsibility.

As we have already seen, our current way of working often places great demands on both our time and our sense of duty. We are expected to down tools and pitch in whenever we are needed and to put in that extra bit of effort whenever that is required. Doing this extra work is rarely presented to us explicitly as an obligation. It comes instead in the form of an appeal to our sense of responsibility and team spirit: 'We are all responsible for making sure this gets done.' And if it doesn't happen, there are usually plenty of people ready to stoke our sense of guilt just to get us on board: 'You don't want to burden your colleagues with all that extra work, do you?'

Employers are often very pleased when you feel overly responsible for your work. It means you can be trusted, are always ready to lend a hand when needed and are able to maintain your focus on the end result. The fact that this also results in a lot of stress on your part is your problem, not theirs. In addition, when you are the one who is always prepared to take responsibility for a certain task, this also creates the expectation that you will do the same again next time around. The more often you voluntarily take on the brunt of the work, the more others will be inclined to sit back and relax. Not only is this exasperating for you, but it also means you deny others the opportunity to shoulder their share of the burden.

Before her burnout Eliza (31) had always had a high sense of responsibility. She now recognises it as one of the reasons why she was flattened by a burnout: 'I was extremely ambitious. I took on everything that I thought wouldn't get done – or not get done well enough – if I didn't do it. I paid no attention whatsoever to whether this was good for me or whether I actually liked the work involved. I assumed responsibility for everything that came my way and that needed – in my opinion – extra work. I eventually ended up with five jobs all rolled into one.'

Since her burnout Eliza has begun to see this character trait in a different light. To do so she has adopted a method from the world of post-delivery. A postman generally has a fairly clear job description: to deliver the post at a certain time in a certain neighbourhood. That's it. The neighbourhood is clearly defined and the postman knows exactly which addresses lie within their patch and which ones don't. If they are asked to do something that relates to a different neighbourhood, they will almost always reply: 'Not my patch, sorry!' The rest of us would be well-advised to adopt this mentality in our own work, too. Yes, employing the postman's attitude might make you a little less popular and raise an eyebrow or two, especially among those who are used to dumping their work on you. But these worries pale in comparison with the sense of peace and calm this approach can create.

There is another method I once learned from a coach. You can use it to quicky determine where your responsibilities lie and where they don't. Whenever you are unsure about whether a particular responsibility is yours or not, ask yourself this question: 'Do I have to do this now?' This simple question can be applied to any request or task. It works like a kind of Inspector Gadget tool: you can break it down into four separate constituent parts, each of which pertains to a different aspect of the question.

The first part is: Do **I** have to do this now? Is my contribution absolutely essential or could I get someone else to do it? (Follow-up question: Is there a smart way of outsourcing the task to someone else?). The second part is: Do I **HAVE TO** do this now? Is it imperative that I take on this task or do I have a choice in the matter? (If you have a choice, ask this question: Do I actually want to take this on?). The third part is: Do I have to do **THIS** now? Would I not be better off spending my time on something more urgent? Is this the best way I can spend my time at this moment? And finally, the fourth part: Do I have to do this **NOW**? Is this really the thing I should be focusing my attention on right now? Does it have to be done now or can it wait until later? Is there something else that is more important?

Do I have to do this now?

Do I HAVE TO do this now?

Do I have to do THIS now?

Do I have to do this NOW?

If your answer to any of the above is 'no', then you don't have to worry about addressing the task immediately.

Take three things you are going to do today and for each one ask the question: Do I have to do this now? If the answer is 'no', then don't do it. To help you to remember, draw a question mark on the back of your hand. If someone asks you why you have a question mark drawn on your hand, it will give you the perfect opportunity to share the technique with them.

## Setting boundaries

 Think back to the last time you found it difficult to say 'no' to something. What was the reason? What made it difficult? What, in retrospect, could you have done differently?

Most of us have a deep desire to be liked by others. As a result, we often find it difficult to say 'no' or to set boundaries. We are usually afraid we might upset the other person if we do. However, it is inevitable that you will encounter situations in which your interests are at odds with the person or circumstance you are facing. If you have followed the principles in this chapter – for example, when the answer to the question 'Do I have to do this now?' is 'no' – it is inevitable that you will have to set boundaries for yourself (and others). Sometimes you simply have to say 'no'. If you always say 'yes' because of a fear of being disliked, you will only end up piling more work on your plate. But how do you say 'no', actually? Here's a quick 5-step course.

**Step 1** The *How to say 'no'* course starts between your ears. Before you say 'no' to something, you have to give yourself permission to do so. Have you the right to say 'no'? Do you have a choice in the matter? Consider the possible consequences of saying 'no'. Would you be able to cope with the other person being very upset, for example? If your answer to these questions is 'yes' – and you can therefore grant yourself permission to say 'no' – you can move on to the next step.

**Step 2** When you have decided to say 'no' it is useful to think about how you are going to say it. A conversation in which you set out your boundaries is best conducted face to face or, if necessary, on the telephone. If you send a text message, the person on the receiving end may miss important information that you can only convey through your tone of voice or physical presence. You should also think about the timing of your message: if you pick a moment when the other person is relaxed and not distracted, they are less likely to fly into a rage. A bit like how I used to approach my father: I quickly learned that it was never clever to ask him a tricky question when he had just come home from work and might be in a bad mood. It was always better to wait until he had been sitting reading the newspaper for half an hour before I approached him.

There are two sides to every message sent between two people: that of the sender and that of the receiver. The message the sender sends is not always the message the receiver receives. It can be distorted on both sides. For example, consider the following message: 'Can you put out the garbage?' The sender can mean several different things with this request. It can mean: 'I don't have time to do it. Can you do it for me?', but it can also be underpinned by a certain emotion: 'Why didn't you think of doing it yourself?' A similar process can also take place at the receiver's end. Such a request may be interpreted as an example of micromanaging or even a sign of distrust: 'You don't need to tell me what to do!'

Generally speaking, you have a lot of control over how you as a sender formulate your message, but you have little control over how the receiver will react. You can try to predict their reaction based on what you already know about them and use that to package your message as judiciously as possible, but you will never know for sure how they will interpret it. They might still become angry when they are on the receiving end of your 'no', with or without good reason. In that case, it might be useful to assume they are angry about your message and not at you personally.

One thing you do have control over, however, is how you transmit your message. There are a number of tricks you can use to ensure that your message comes across clearly but not aggressively.

Step 3 is all about diplomacy. You should try to package your message in such a way that it relates primarily to you. When you do so the receiver is less likely to interpret it as being critical of them. Let's take a simple example: someone asks you if you can attend a meeting, but you actually have better things to be doing. 'I hate to turn you down, but I'm afraid this time I will have to decline' sounds a lot more diplomatic than 'You keep on inviting me to these stupid meetings, even though you know I don't have the time!'

The biggest potential pitfall when you want to say 'no' is allowing last-minute doubt to creep in at the critical moment, causing you to give in, in spite of your resolve. You can avoid this by taking the necessary time to prepare beforehand. It's useful to make a detailed plan for what you are going to say and how you will say it. Stick to your message as much as you can. Try to anticipate the receiver's reaction, too, and what your own reaction should be. Write down your message – in no more than 20 words, the simpler the better – and practice saying it out loud. The better you prepare your message, the smaller the risk that you will end up diluting it.

The real professionals know how to say no and still leave the receiver feeling good about themselves. Try to find ways in which you can pay someone a compliment while simultaneously saying 'no': 'This sounds great and I'm very flattered by your request. Normally I wouldn't hesitate to say yes, but I just can't squeeze it into my diary at the moment. But I'm sure you'll find someone else for this terrific project!'

**Step 4** is damage control. You may know in advance that your 'no' is not going to be warmly received and that you are facing a difficult conversation because you have to say 'no' to someone you know to be a persuasive character and used to engaging in discussion. You might expect them to fly into a rage or start arguing before you have had the time to fully explain your reasons.

In such cases you can make use of a technique that doctors employ when they have to give a patient bad news: convey the message clearly first – and as neutrally as you can – before explaining the details. There are two advantages to this strategy. Firstly, it ensures that you get your message across loud and clear so that there can be no misunderstanding. Secondly, it offers the receiver some time to allow the message to sink in.

An example: 'You asked if I could work some extra hours. Unfortunately, that's just not possible at the moment. [Silent pause] That's mostly because . . .'

The reason you should pause after conveying your message is because it allows you to separate your decision ('no!') from the reasons for that decision. This way you present your final decision as exactly that: final and not up for discussion. If you want, you can also give your reasons but your decision is set in stone.[5] If you don't pause for a moment, the other person may believe they can still change your mind by endlessly discussing your reasons until you decide to give in. Of course, you can show sympathy for the receiver's position and acknowledge their emotions, but don't let them make you go back on your own decision.

**Step 5** It is quite possible that, despite your best efforts to be diplomatic, your 'no' just won't be accepted easily. You might even meet some serious resistance. Unfortunately, sometimes there's just no avoiding the fact that 'haters gonna hate'. No matter how carefully you prepare and convey your message, some people will be aggrieved or disappointed, especially when they secretly expected you to bow to their wishes without argument. Be prepared for this eventuality as well. And if you find yourself being ambushed by the other party, you are always entitled to take whatever time you need to think things through: 'I need to think about this for a while. Let me get back to you tomorrow.'

Setting boundaries is something you do for yourself, not for others. You will inevitably meet some resistance, no matter how diplomatic you are. It is impossible to stand up for yourself and stay on friendly terms with everyone at the same time. Conflict is sometimes unavoidable when you stand your ground.

You can be as diplomatic as you like about how you say 'no' but not everyone will appreciate it. However, you are not obliged to appease others, especially when they are not willing to accept 'no' as an answer. If you meet someone who continually refuses to respect your boundaries, the best thing is to eliminate them. No, I'm not suggesting you hire a hitman. Just avoid that person as much as you possibly can. But what if it is a friend? Then maybe your friendship has run its course. A colleague at work? Try to avoid working together with them when you can. Your manager? You'd be better off working with someone who is willing to cooperate. And if it's your partner? Well, good luck!

Now that you have been introduced to the 5-step *How to say 'no'* course, I have one small request. Please read this chapter again, just so you can implant these steps firmly in your brain. What's that I hear? You don't want to? Well done, you have just passed the course with flying colours.

## Choosing a more relaxed life

You can choose to lead a less busy and hectic life and this can be done by tackling some of the psychological habits and patterns we have addressed in this chapter. A more relaxed life starts in your mind and requires you to think differently about certain things. You first have to realise you're allowed to make choices. And when you also realise you can say 'no' and know how to do that effectively, you will be well on your way.

There is a chance, of course, that not everyone around you will be happy when you decide to apply these techniques. It may be that the people with whom you work and live have become used to expecting you to do everything perfectly and take responsibility for things that are not your responsibility at all. You may have inadvertently created the expectation that you can be called upon at any moment to solve other people's problems. So it can come as quite a shock to them when this is no longer the case. You may also meet with some resistance. And some people will like you less as a result. Always remember to ask yourself this question: who do I put first, myself or everybody else? Regardless of how you answer this, the choice is always yours.

You can create a less chaotic mind by:

- eliminating 'I have to' and taking control of your own life;
- eliminating or outsourcing tasks instead of putting them off until the last minute (procrastination eats up heaps of energy);
- knowing when something has to be 100% perfect and when 'good enough' is really good enough;
- knowing what falls under your responsibility and, more crucially, what doesn't;
- being prepared to set boundaries and to say 'no' when you need to.

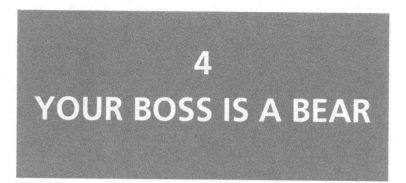

# 4
# YOUR BOSS IS A BEAR

'Stress' has become a popular word in our vocabulary. We refer to certain circumstances as 'stressful' ('Barry works in The City, so he must be under a lot of stress!'), regard it as a character trait among others ('Amber is always stressed out!') or believe that certain things invariably end up causing stress ('I wore one of those fitness trackers for a week but all it did was tell me I wasn't moving around enough. The result? More stress!'). We tend to see stress as something that simply comes with the territory in certain situations or types of people. But is that really the case?

According to the experts, stress is a 'a physical and psychological reaction to a stressor.' In other words, something that happens in both the brain and the body when you are faced with a stressful situation. Think of the feeling you get when you discover you've lost your wallet. The stressor in this case is the possibility that you have lost a wad of cash and all your bank cards. Your body reacts by switching to survival mode until you have found your wallet again (or solved the problem in some other way). Stressors come in all shapes and sizes. So, in order to understand what happens in a stressful situation, we need to look at what goes on in the brain and in the body.

## Hormones and the nervous system

When you encounter a stressor your head and body switch to alarm mode. This is an involuntary reaction: you never have to think about how to react to a stressful situation, you just do so automatically. You often only become aware of your reaction after it has already kicked in. By that time your brain has already taken a number of different steps.

This reaction to stress has two phases. The first one – the fast phase – relates to how your nervous system responds. Your nervous system is made up of your brain cells and the neurons that connect your brain to the rest of your body via your spine. It controls your organs and muscles and allows you to experience the world through your senses. It enables you to hold a book in your hands, dictates how your eyes follow the letters on this page and allows you to understand what the author is trying to tell you. At the same time, it makes sure you continue breathing without ever having to think about it (except for now).

Your nervous system has two modes: the parasympathetic mode and the sympathetic mode. When we are relaxed the nervous system is in parasympathetic mode. In this mode our digestive system can work efficiently, our immune system is at its strongest, wounds can heal and waste products can be ejected from the body. However, when we are faced with a dangerous or life-threatening situation the sympathetic mode kicks in. The sympathetic nervous system allows us to react in a matter of milliseconds and it also produces the stress hormone adrenaline. If you have ever done anything exciting just for the sake of the kick it gives you – a ride in a rollercoaster or a parachute jump – then you know the effect adrenaline can have: it makes you active and switches you on like nothing else.

The second, much slower phase of your reaction to stress kicks in after a few minutes. The brain produces certain types of hormones that in turn produce cortisol in your adrenal cortex. Your body produces cortisol 24 hours a day, but during times of stress the rate of production goes through the roof. Cortisol ensures that your brain and body have enough fuel to be able to cope with long periods of stress. Too much cortisol, however, can adversely affect your memory and your immune system and can trigger an urge to consume more fats and sugar.

## Fight or flight

When the adrenaline is coursing through your veins, your body undergoes a whole host of changes. The amount of energy at your disposal skyrockets because there is more glucose available as fuel. Your heart starts beating faster and your blood pressure goes up. Your breathing becomes shallower and more rapid. Blood begins to flow to your arms and legs and your muscles get ready to spring into action. Your digestive system shuts down in order to save precious energy. In other words, the body's resources are redistributed so that you can react to danger as quickly as possible. All non-essential functions are suspended and your energy is focused only on those things that will ensure your survival. If you happen to pick up an injury in the heat of the moment, you will probably only notice it when your adrenaline level has gone down again because of the effect stress hormones have on your perception and tolerance of pain.

More fuel is sent to the brain, too, and you quickly notice the effect. If you had been feeling tired, the fatigue disappears in a flash. You are suddenly full of energy, completely focused and your brain goes into overdrive. You may feel slightly agitated or even panicky and susceptible to tunnel vision. You react quickly to warning signs in your immediate surroundings. Your brain also readies itself to respond immediately to dangerous situations: Run, NOW!

All the stuff that happens in your body and in your brain is no accident either. The mechanism comes from a time when humans were confronted with dangerous situations on a regular basis. Today we are used to living in a safer environment, but life was a lot different for our ancestors, who had to face danger every single day. If they went out picking berries, there was a good chance they would run into a bear. And at night they could be paid a surprise visit by a hostile tribe. In those kinds of situations keeping a cool head was of paramount importance and thanks to our stress system humans have always had the capacity to do so.

I recently went on a trip to a rainforest in Asia. One evening I was sitting outside my tent reading a book when something hit my head. It was an insect the size of my fist that had been attracted by the lights in the camp. One moment I was relaxing on a bench with my book and the next I was shouting like a madman and waving my book frantically around in the air in an attempt to ward off the intruder. All of this happened automatically, I didn't have to think about it for one second. It was as if some kind of primal instinct had taken control of me.

This response forms part of our survival mode and it allows us to react to dangerous situations without having to take the time to think. It makes sure our body and brain are ready to fight or flee. The physical changes that occur enable us to either stand and fight or run away as fast as we can, depending on the best course of action. And when your brain decides that neither fighting nor running is a good option, there is a third possibility: freeze. In that case the body reacts by going completely still so as not to attract attention – a proven method when confronted with a wild animal. This is why we sometimes find ourselves frozen to the spot and unable to utter a word in perilous situations.

It doesn't take a genius to conclude that those of our ancestors who were able to react quickly to danger were more likely to live longer. As a result, their genes were passed down to the next generation. Early humans who believed that the best course of action was to discuss the situation with the bear never lived live long enough to procreate.

## Cave dweller with an office job

Our evolutionary alarm system is an excellent tool when we need to rescue ourselves from the jaws of danger. It enables us to respond adequately when in peril, for example by activating our defences when we cross paths with a bear. This happens all by itself and it requires no conscious action on our part. Sounds extremely useful, until you realise that today the very same alarm system often causes us more problems than it prevents.

We now live in secure environments that are generally safe and peaceful. You could say that the pace of our cultural evolution has far outstripped that of our physical evolution over the past few thousand years. Instead of wandering around in the jungle looking for berries, we are now more used to the concrete jungle of the office environment. We have swapped our battles with hostile tribes for those with colleagues, clients and the tax authorities. We make less use of our muscles and rely more on our diplomatic skills. And the bear we are most likely to encounter comes in the form of our boss.

Our alarm system has not been able to keep up with these developments. We may live our lives now as modern humans with a house, a refrigerator and public transport, but to our stress system we are still no more than a primitive cave dweller. Our body reacts to the 'dangerous' situations we face today – like having to give a presentation or going for a job interview – in exactly the same way as it has always done. Which is not terribly useful really, because instead of running away what we mostly need to do nowadays is to think our way out of trouble. And that's never easy when you're standing there trembling like a leaf from all the stress.

Our stress system is not exactly superbly equipped to deal with our current way of life. And as if that didn't make things difficult enough, there is another problem too. After our cave-dwelling ancestors had managed to extricate themselves from a perilous situation with a bear, they usually became their old, relaxed selves again within a few minutes. Their alarm system only had to be activated for a short period of time (and if they didn't manage to escape, their stress reaction came to its own abrupt end anyway, for obvious reasons). However, if they were able to escape up a tree or even get the better of the bear, then everything quickly returned to normal. The parasympathetic nervous system took control and allowed the body to relax, and our ancestors to put their feet up. The stress was followed by a period of recovery so that the cave dweller could recharge and move on again.

In our modern-day lives we get stressed about other kinds of things and for longer periods, too. If you have an interview coming up for your dream job on Friday, you will probably start worrying about it on Monday. Our hectic and fleeting existence is the cause of so many stressors that we often end up stuck in alarm mode. We are constantly bombarded with things that cause us stress, which makes it extremely difficult to switch off the alarm and allow ourselves to rest. It is not easy to relax when you are permanently in survival mode.

> How do you know when you are in alarm mode? Is it a feeling or a thought or is it something in your behaviour? And how do you know you are truly relaxed? When does that happen?

Having a certain amount of stress in your life is unavoidable and is, in fact, actually good for you. It's what gets you fired up to produce the work needed to meet your deadline and puts you 'in the zone' when you have to give an important presentation. This sort of stress is commonly known as 'healthy tension'. But intense or prolonged periods of stress are bad for your health, especially for your heart and blood vessels, respiratory system, brain, and mental and emotional well-being.

In short, getting stuck too often and for too long in your alarm mode is very damaging for your health. There is a limit to the amount of stress your body and mind are able to tolerate in the long term. And if you subject yourself to too much stress and ignore all the warning signs, you run the risk of suffering a burnout, a subject we will be discussing in more detail in the next chapter.

## Stressors

The total amount of stress we experience from day to day is the sum of all the stress we encounter in all the different areas in our lives. It is undeniable that our lives have become more stressful in all of those areas (work, social life, relationships, etc.). A person with a very demanding job but who can relax sufficiently in the private sphere is much better off than someone who is under strain both at work and at home.

Stress can also be the result of an external factor. Most of us encounter stressors regularly at work: targets that are beyond your reach, angry customers, impossible deadlines, a permanently overflowing mailbox or the fear of losing your job when a reorganisation is announced. Having to give a presentation is also a major stressor for many people. In fact, 'speaking in public' ranks higher than 'dying' in the top 10 of people's fears. I am reminded of a bad joke some psychologists like to tell: when we attend a funeral, many of us would prefer to be in the coffin than have to go up to the pulpit and speak.

We also run into a lot of stressors outside our work: family trouble, problems with your partner and noisy neighbours. Raising children also has its fair share of stressors, like when you are tying the shoelaces of uncooperative child A while exasperating child B is flinging his breakfast around the kitchen.

Yet another category of stressors – technostress – finds its origins in our telephones, laptops, tablets and smart TVs. As Tyler Durden puts it in the cult film *Fight Club* (1999), 'The things you own end up owning you.' While these technological wonders may enrich our lives, they are also the cause of much agitation and stress, even when they are doing what you actually want them to do. There are also plenty of times when these devices tug annoyingly at our sleeves because they need an update, back-up or upgrade. And they have an irritating habit, too, of not working precisely when you need them the most.

Contrary to what you might expect, the things that can cause us prolonged stress (marital break-up, a death in the family, bankruptcy) do not always have a negative tint. The list of most stressful experiences also includes getting married, moving to a new home, starting your own business and reaching retirement age. Whether negative or positive, every major change in life has an enormous impact on us and tests our ability to adapt.

The final category consists of psychological factors – the stressors inside your head: worrying about others, about your appearance or about what other people think of you; negative self-evaluation ('I should be well able to do this! I'm such an ass!'); concerns about your health or that of someone close to you; and worrying about your finances or your future. It is also worth noting that we are more prone to stress when we have slept badly, are hungry or are feeling run-down.

> Make a list of your biggest stressors. Consider not only the things related to your work but also your personal life, social life, family, relations, techno-stress, etc. For each stressor write down the answer to this question: why does this cause me stress?

## Baseline stress level

There is another cruel joke that Mother Nature likes to play on us: the more stressed out we are, the easier it is to become even more stressed. This is because of the way our tension levels build up. All the stress that you experience in a day or week gradually builds up inside you, especially when you don't fully recover between bouts of stress. The more stress you endure, the higher your baseline stress level becomes. And the higher your baseline, the more stressed you will react to events around you.

Picture the following scenario. You receive an e-mail at work from an unsatisfied customer who has a complaint to make about you. The alarm bells immediately go off and your body starts producing adrenaline and cortisol. As a result, your heart starts beating faster, you are unable to think clearly and you feel a state of panic coming on, but somehow you manage to keep everything under control. However, it also means that you are feeling very tense when you go into your next meeting with your manager, who then proceeds to tell you that the deadline for the project you are working on has been brought forward by a week. Under normal circumstances this would be no real cause for concern, but because you are already stressed out you find yourself starting to worry: is this do-able? Later, on your way home, a car pulls out suddenly in front of you and you have to do your best not to jump out from behind the wheel and give the driver a piece of your mind. When you finally get home, your partner asks you a prickly question and you completely lose it.

This scenario describes a number of stressors that may not generate much stress individually, but when you experience them all in quick succession they pile up and can send your stress level through the roof. In this case it is not one big stressor that does the damage but a host of smaller ones all bunched together. This explains why people sometimes worry excessively about seemingly trivial matters when their stress level is high. The higher your baseline stress level, the greater the risk that you will become even more stressed out by the next stressor. In short, stress often leads to even more stress.

How high is your baseline stress level on a scale of 1 to 10? '1' is completely relaxed, '10' is riddled with stress.

Picture an elastic band. When at rest it is very flexible. If you pull on it, the rubber gives easily. When you let go it returns to its former state very quickly. However, if you stretch the band for a long period of time it will begin to lose its elasticity. The rubber may even become damaged. Eventually, the elastic band will most likely break, even when stretched just a little.

The same applies to your stress level. If your baseline is way too high to begin with, the consequences can be very serious and you may be in danger of wearing yourself out. If you don't have a way of relieving this basic tension on a regular basis – for example by doing breathing exercises, getting enough rest or doing yoga and some other relaxing activity – any small stressor will send you into a panic. You are explosive material, ready to blow.

You could think of your baseline stress level in terms of the colour code that meteorologists often use to describe the weather. If your level is green, then things would have to go terribly wrong to put you off balance. You are well able to deal with upsets and solve the problems that come your way. When your level moves to yellow a major setback has the potential to push you badly off course. Code orange means that it doesn't take much to push you over the edge – a misplaced remark can be enough to send you into a spin. And when you find yourself in the red zone, your baseline stress level is so high that even the slightest hiccup can reduce you to a blubbering mess.

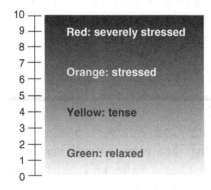

    Keep track of your baseline stress level for one week. You can do this by setting an alarm to go off at different times of the day. When the alarm sounds, rank on a scale of 1 to 10 (see above) how high your stress level is at that moment. After a week a pattern will emerge that shows when your stress level is at its highest and lowest.

## Breathe

Are you shocked by what you have read up to this point about the negative effects of stress? If so, draw a deep breath – it really helps.

    What is your breathing like right now? Are you breathing deeply from your abdomen or is your breath high in your chest?

There are different ways of bringing your stress levels down. You can go for a walk, preferably in nature; you can ask someone to listen while you express your concerns; you can do something relaxing, like reading a book (which you are doing right now – good for you!); or you could spend some time playing with your cat or dog. All of these can help to reduce your stress level. However, the easiest way to bring your baseline stress level down is by breathing.

You are normally not aware of how you breathe. It is an automatic process, it happens all by itself. When you exert yourself (for example, when you take exercise) your heart rate goes up and your breathing becomes faster. The opposite is true when you are relaxed. And when you are asleep your breathing is slow and regular.

When the alarm bells are going off inside you, however, your breathing becomes rapid and shallow. Your body adjusts itself to this new, higher stress level but you can bring that level back down again by changing the way you breathe. This forces your body to shut down the stress response. Regular, slow breathing is also associated with a more efficient immune system, improved heart function and deeper relaxation. The easiest way to achieve this is by *breathing more slowly*.

If you are under pressure or feeling stressed, you tend to take around ten to twelve breaths per minute and sometimes more. For most people, between six and eight breaths per minute is ideal for achieving a relaxed state. You can reduce the tempo of your breathing by making sure that you exhale longer than you inhale. This will reduce the number of breaths you take within a matter of minutes. Don't try to force it, it should feel easy and natural. If it doesn't, then you are trying to adjust your breathing too quickly. At first, slowing your breathing down may feel a bit weird. It's a bit like driving a car: when you leave the motorway and have to reduce your speed to 50 km/hr, it can feel unnaturally slow for a moment or two. But when you get used to it the slower speed doesn't seem strange anymore.

Another technique involves holding your breath for a few seconds before breathing out again. Known as the 4-7-8 technique, it comes from a practice in yoga called pranayama: breathe in through your nose for four seconds, hold your breath for seven seconds and breathe out through your mouth for eight seconds. If you don't feel like counting and breathing at the same time, there are plenty of apps you can use to time your breathing.

This exercise is great when you are feeling tense. Sit down on a comfortable chair. Use your watch or smartphone to keep track of your breathing. Take a few minutes to slow your breathing down to 6–8 breaths per minute. How do you feel now?

Conscious breathing is a very effective way of bringing the stress response down to a manageable level. In the following chapters we will discuss more tips and techniques that can help you to combat stress. In Chapter 6 (Warning!) you will find a complete step-by-step plan for coping with extreme stress. In chapters 7 (Peace of Mind) and 8 (Focused on the Job) we will examine what you can do to prevent stress from arising in the first place.

We suffer greatly from stress nowadays because:

- our stress system stems from a time when it had to decide how to react to a dangerous situation in a matter of milliseconds: fight, flight or freeze;
- there is a mismatch between this kind of fight-or-flight reaction and the types of situations that cause us stress nowadays;
- we spend too much time stuck in 'alarm mode';
- modern life forces us to deal with different kinds of stressors that often lead to much longer periods of stress;
- the combined stressors in our work and personal lives often make our baseline stress level quite high, causing us to become stressed even quicker when we are faced with a stressor.

5
BURNOUT

Burnout is the catchword of our times. Whereas ten years ago the term was used rather sparingly, in 2022 burnout is on everybody's lips. It is to be found in the news, in magazines and at every coffee corner. It affects not only those who have been working in their chosen careers for years but also newly-fledged professionals and students. Today there is an abundance of burnout coaches, special expertise centres, self-help books and TV programmes. Vloggers, musicians, writers and top athletes are now more than willing to share their personal stories about burning out.

Burnout is becoming a more and more common occurrence. Around half of all employees in the US say that they have difficulty handling their workload. The potential cost to society is nothing short of frightening. A third of all those deemed unfit to work in the UK have had to stop working because of a burnout or stress-related issues. In my own country, the Netherlands, each burnout is estimated to cost €60,000 per year in terms of medical expenses and absenteeism. In the US, stress and burnout are now costing businesses around $300 billion a year in health care costs, absenteeism and falling productivity. The financial aspects of our burnout-inducing working culture are not the main concern, however. The biggest price is that paid by the individuals who suffer a burnout: months and sometimes years spent on the sidelines and in recovery. It all adds up to a monstrous waste of talent and capital.

Up until quite recently it was widely believed that only those whose personality did not suit their work in some way or other suffered a burnout. It was thought they were simply too conscientious, too neurotic, too anxious or 'weak', and so it was only 'logical' that they would suffer a burnout from doing the kind of work that 'normal' people could do without any trouble. Fortunately we now look at the matter in a much different light and the reality is that anyone can suffer a burnout. It is part and parcel of our modern, hectic way of life. It is not the people who suffer a burnout who are at fault, but the way in which we have become accustomed to working and living.

In his book *Borderline Times* the Belgian psychiatrist Dirk de Wachter compares modern-day society to a speedboat, one that is moving ever faster. Both society and technology are developing at an increasingly faster pace. As a result, the demands placed on us are growing, too. The faster the speedboat travels, the tighter the passengers must hold on to avoid being thrown overboard. Some eventually lose their grip and disappear under the water, not because they are not strong enough or clever enough but simply because of the speed at which the boat is travelling.

Burnouts are now an accepted part of modern life. The pressure to perform is so high that we often lose the run of ourselves. We live in extremely busy times, so it is no wonder that many of us fall victim to stress. However, this does not mean that burnout has become widely acknowledged and accepted in society. Despite all the celebrities who are keen to share their burnout experiences, in many sectors the phenomenon is still very much taboo. In fact, there is still a lot of stigma attached to burnout and people who suffer a burnout often have to wrestle with feelings of personal failure and guilt.

If you end up suffering a burnout, it's worth remembering that you are not the only one and that you have not gone mad. In a very real sense, you are simply unfortunate to have fallen victim to the curse of our times. It is not something you need to be ashamed of or should blame yourself for. You are not a loser. And here's something else you should keep in mind: no matter how awful it is, many eventually regard their burnout experience as a very educational and meaningful one.

In this chapter we will discuss what a burnout is exactly, how it affects you and how you can recover. We will follow the experiences of Eliza, Puck and Marco, and we will look at one of the underlying causes of many burnouts: being stuck in your head so much you lose the connection with the rest of your body.

## What is a burnout?

I meet Puck (29) in a café where they sell 22 different kinds of tea. She has just come from her yoga class ('We did the sixth and seventh chakras this morning') and orders a pot of Chinese Tree Bark tea. Puck lives a full and busy life. She is a serious gaming expert, a consultant for several different organisations and a lecturer in intercultural communication – all at the same time. She fills her free time with a wide variety of activities and dedicates whatever time she has left to designing table-top games. She juggles so many different things that she often loses sight of the bigger picture, as she readily admits herself. Last year she suffered her first burnout.

Puck had been sleeping badly: 'I would lie awake worrying about stuff and rarely fell asleep before 5 a.m. Three hours of sleep for two weeks in a row was too much to bear. I turned into a zombie.' Getting up in the morning after yet another sleepless night became harder and harder. Her boss became suspicious when she sent an e-mail to her team at work at five o'clock in the morning. He sent her a stern message ('Puck, turn off your laptop and telephone. Now!') and made an appointment for her to see the doctor at work. They concluded that she was suffering from a burnout and advised her to take a break from work.

Looking back now, Puck wonders how she managed to miss the warning signs. In the months leading up to her burnout she was 'an emotional wreck'. At work she appeared to be full of energy and good-humoured, but at home she was a 'small pile of misery'. She didn't have the energy to do even the simplest things: 'Even the smallest tasks felt like climbing Mount Everest.' When she had the flu she went to see her doctor and got very angry when he told her to take it easy: 'What do you mean "take it easy"? I've already been off work for TWO DAYS! What do you expect me to do?!'

A burnout is the last stop on a person's stress journey. It is usually preceded by a long period of excessive stress (or a short period of extreme stress). In that period a person's normal stress level has become so high that they find it impossible to relax. When you find yourself in this position it is extremely difficult to carry on working and get enough rest at the same time. When your stress system is activated so often that it gets to a point where you cannot deactivate it anymore, we call that a burnout.

A burnout can be described as an 'injury' to the stress system. The system that regulates your stress levels – and normally takes you out of alarm mode – is dealt such a heavy blow that it ceases to function properly. It becomes damaged and remains in the 'on' position. A burnout snaps the elastic that has been struggling with the strain for too long.

Your baseline stress level remains high as a result. As long as you're in this state, the smallest things stress you out and it becomes increasingly difficult to get rid of the feeling. This is why someone with a burnout finds it so hard to perform even the most basic tasks, like shopping for groceries or cleaning the house.

Compare this injury to your stress system with a physical injury to your biceps, for instance. Given the proper instruction, you can train your biceps to lift a substantial weight. You achieve this by training regularly, steadily increasing the weight and taking enough rest in between. However, if you train irresponsibly and try to lift too much weight too soon or make the wrong kind of movement, you run the risk of injuring yourself. Once the muscle has been injured you will not be able to put it under any strain at all for a certain period of time. Only after taking plenty of rest will you be able to start training the muscle again. And if you haven't learned your lesson and try lifting too much weight too quickly, chances are you will suffer an even worse injury.

The same happens with a burnout. Normally, your stress system is able to manage some strain – as long as you take enough time to recover between bouts of stress. However, should you overtax your system by trying to do too much in too short a space of time without taking the proper rest, you will end up overtraining your stress muscle and eventually injuring it. Once you reach this burnout stage you will be forced to avoid all strenuous mental effort and give your system lots of recovery time – whether you want to or not. Only when you have rested well enough – building your energy slowly – will you be able to handle your responsibilities again at work and in your personal life.

Burnout is not the same as extreme fatigue, although the two often get confused. Extreme fatigue is actually the stage *before* burnout. When you're suffering from extreme fatigue you can still adjust your workload to avoid reaching the burnout stage. It is possible to take action to prevent it from getting worse. Once you reach the point of burnout, however, you no longer have that option. The only thing you can do is accept the situation for what it is and embark on a long period of recovery.

Eliza (31) suffered a burnout just after she had her first child. At the time she was also in the middle of both a home renovation project and a reorganisation at work. No matter what she did she could never get enough sleep. That's always a challenge with a new-born baby, of course, but in Eliza's case it went beyond the normal new parent stress. She found herself constantly worrying when she was trying to get some shut-eye. Eating also became difficult. The amount of physical tension she was feeling meant she could barely swallow a morsel of food. When she watched TV she found it impossible to pay attention to whatever programme was on. Her head was always in a spin, which caused her to overreact to almost every impulse: 'Everything felt like a potential threat, to both me and my child. I felt like I was going crazy. I was a complete wreck.'

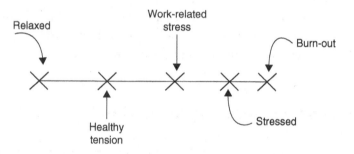

Sometimes a burnout can be caused by a single, extremely stressful situation, but more often than not – as in Eliza's case – it is the end result of a long period of stress in your life. This often comes as a surprise to the person in question: 'I wasn't under any more stress than normal, was I?' Maybe not, but that 'normal' turned out to be so stressful that Eliza ended up depleting all of her reserves until there was nothing left in the tank.

The stress in our lives is the sum of all the stressors we experience in our daily activities: the demands that our job, domestic situation, family life, health and social life place on us. As we've seen in previous chapters, personal factors (for example, whether you are a perfectionist or burdened with a heavy sense of responsibility) also play a role.

When there is too much stress in one area of your life you are usually able to handle it, but when the stress levels are high in both your working and personal life things can start to get dangerous very quickly. This explains why some people suffer a burnout and others don't (under the same circumstances). Your personality, your baseline level of stress and the way you organise your life – they can all make you more or less vulnerable. But regardless of whether your individual circumstances have blessed you with a long or a short elastic, it can always break when the strain becomes too much.

## How do you recognise a burnout?

No two burnouts are the same. This can make it very difficult to recognise one. A burnout displays similarities with depression, post-traumatic stress syndrome and chronic fatigue. It also tends to be accompanied by a wide range of physical symptoms, including sore muscles, sensitivity to sounds and other stimuli, and headaches.

A burnout is said to be characterised by (1) feelings of exhaustion, (2) increased mental distance (or increased negativism or cynicism) in relation to one's work and (3) reduced productivity.[6] However, there is still a lack of clarity with regard to this diagnosis. Diagnostic manuals tend to focus on burnout from a work perspective and ignore stress that is more related to the personal sphere. The exact boundaries of the diagnosis are also unclear: for example, do you have to be absent from your work for a certain period of time before you can qualify for the diagnosis?'

One thing for certain is that a burnout is almost always preceded by a period of extreme stress. It usually affects people who have pushed their body and mind too far for too long; those who have demanded too much of themselves, have not taken enough rest or have pandered to the needs of others for too long. A burnout is often your body's way of forcing you to stop and take a break.

Stress-related complaints can almost always be traced back to a protracted period of physical or mental fatigue or increased levels of fatigue as a result of mental exertion. Extreme fatigue can therefore act as a warning sign. The following symptoms can also be a sign of excessive stress: muscle pain in the back and neck, tension, panic, despondency, headache, irritation, lack of concentration, absence of enjoyment and motivation, dizziness, sleep problems, stomach problems and an inability to relax. It can also be accompanied by emotional exhaustion (the feeling that you can't go on), a detached and cynical attitude towards your work and colleagues and the feeling that you always come up short. If you are experiencing these symptoms (and they cannot be attributed to an underlying condition) and they are making your life difficult (because you are unable to work, for example), then you may be suffering from a burnout.

Marco (26) was full of enthusiasm when he started his apprenticeship as a reporter for a radio station. Like many of his other activities – running a drama group, working out three times a week, writing his thesis – he threw himself wholeheartedly into this new challenge. In the first few weeks of his apprenticeship he contributed one great news story after another. A couple of weeks later, however, the inspiration dried up. He began to fall behind in his work and his nervous and irritated behaviour got him into arguments with his colleagues. During an evaluation he and his boss decided it would be best if they terminated his contract.

Around the same time, Marco suffered his first panic attack. He was standing in the changing rooms at a department store when suddenly everything went black before his eyes. He began to hyperventilate. 'I couldn't get out of the place fast enough,' he says. 'I tore off the clothes I had been trying on and raced out the door.' The panic attack was a clear sign for Marco that something had to change: 'I went to bed and didn't get up again for days. I couldn't even eat. All I could do was try to get some rest and recover.'

One of the most remarkable aspects of the stories told by people who have suffered a burnout is that they all seem to miss the early warning signs, however clear they are in hindsight. Eliza kept going until she simply couldn't carry on anymore, Puck's boss had to step in and order her to take a rest. And Marco had to have a panic attack before he decided to take action. Marco: 'I always believed I could never have a burnout. That only ever happened to people much older than me!'

Still, it is not all that strange that we fail to take action until it's too late. We tend to be a lot harder on ourselves than we are on others and prefer to tell ourselves to 'man up' rather than reveal our vulnerability. We tell ourselves to carry on, that everything will sort itself out in the end. When we are stressed we find it harder to make decisions, including those related to our own well-being, and we are more likely to soldier on and continue making poor choices with regard to our health.

It often takes someone else – a friend, family member, your boss, a colleague, a doctor or a psychologist – to show you what's wrong and to step on the brakes. Often, the level of stress has become so normal for the person in question that they simply can't see the problem. Someone else, on the other hand, can view things from the outside and see how stressed the person has become. So if someone tells you that you have a hunted look about you and come across as very stressed, you really should take them seriously – you might just have developed a serious blind spot.

Do you think there are people who are worried about you? Have you perhaps strayed into the danger zone? If so, you need to swallow your pride and ask for help from your friends or family or your boss at work, preferably before you reach the burnout stage. If you are worried about your own stress levels, you may need to slow down and go see your doctor or psychologist. The worst thing you can do is deny everything and rely on your willpower to struggle through, with all the risk that involves.

## Past the shame

After you have been forced to stop working because of a burnout, there will follow a period of anywhere from a few weeks to a couple of months in which you will have to rest as much as possible. Your injured stress system simply needs to recover. In the beginning you will probably find it difficult to do many of the things people are normally able to do: watch TV, for example, or concentrate on a conversation. Your stress level will stay very high for a while. Sometimes even going to the shops is too tall an order.

For many people it is not the physical symptoms of a burnout that are the most difficult aspect but rather the trouble they have accepting the situation. When you suffer a burnout you will be confronted with your own boundaries. You quickly find out that there is a limit to what you are capable of. You may feel like a failure, like you are letting everyone down, including, and especially, yourself.

Puck also had great difficulty accepting her situation. In the first phase of her burnout she found it hard to come to terms with the fact that she had been stopped in her tracks by her own limitations. She was shocked to discover that she wasn't the superwoman she always thought she was. She couldn't find the concentration to read, so she just stared out the window all day thinking. A lot. When she began to feel a bit stronger she tried to use her own wits to recover from her burnout 'as quickly as possible': 'I told myself I had to become really good at recovering from my burnout – as if that was something I should also excel at. My table was littered with self-help books, and lots of dirty cups and plates, too. I knew exactly which phases my burnout would go through. I said to myself, "If I get a lot of sleep for the next two weeks, I will be able to tackle one more thing the following week." It became an obsession.'

Feelings of powerlessness, denial and disappointment are common in the first phase of a burnout. It usually takes a while to accept the fact that you are not able to do as much as you thought you could. With that often comes an overwhelming sense of guilt, as Eliza found out: 'I felt guilty about every single idle moment because I felt I should I have been at work. Slowly but surely, however, I realised that I had a right to just "be" and to "live"; I didn't have to prove myself through my work. I mean, it's not rocket science. How on earth did I not see that earlier?'

One thing that helped Eliza greatly was getting an official diagnosis. It was only after her doctor had officially labelled her burnout that she could accept what had happened to her. Before that she had regarded herself primarily as 'crazy'. 'That's the great thing about a diagnosis – all of a sudden the thing has a name.'

The fact that a burnout leaves you unable to do very much means that you inevitably end up taking a long, hard look at yourself. You are forced to deal with difficult emotions like guilt and shame. You typically reassess your own identity, not in terms of your work or obligations but in terms of your own self-worth. It is only when you are able to see your own intrinsic value outside of your work and achievements – even when you are feeling weak and vulnerable – that the process of recovery can begin in earnest.

## Recovering from burnout

After going through the initial phase of a burnout in which you are required to stop and take stock, you will probably feel up to a little more exertion in the next phase. Try to do stuff that provides you with energy without too much effort, such as going for a walk or reading, if you are able.

The biggest mistake you can make when recovering from a burnout is to want too much too quickly. Many try to go back to work as quickly as they can because they think, 'I was well able to do this before, wasn't I?' Or: 'My colleagues can all manage, so why can't I?' This, however, is a mindset that will make it far more likely for you to suffer a relapse. Unfortunately, many burnouts are characterised by periods of partial recovery followed by relapses into old behaviour.

Recovering from a burnout is a long and time-consuming process. But it is crucial that you take the time to recover properly and not to bite off more than you can chew. Your body will recover from the injury to its stress system and gradually get used to normal activity again. It is a delicate balancing act: on the one hand you are forced to do less than you would like, while on the other you have to test the limits of what you are capable of at any given moment.

Puck's burnout lasted five months, with many peaks and troughs. Important elements of her recovery included a mindfulness course, daily walks in nature and the creation of a weekly 'Puck Day' when she allowed herself to do the things she enjoyed most, like criss-crossing the country on a train with a good book.

Marco wasn't able to find the rest he needed at home because there were too many distractions. Acting on his psychologist's advice, he decided to move to new surroundings for a while.

An exchange project offered him the opportunity to travel to Slovakia. 'I ended up staying in a cabin in the woods where no one could disturb me. Almost no internet and zero distractions, apart from a spot of fishing every now and then. It was only then that I was able to relax.'

Eliza took several drastic measures in her attempt to emerge from her burnout. She decided to stop watching TV and reading the newspaper – cold turkey. She maintained a strict regimen. She went to bed very early and at the same time every evening, made sure she got enough sleep and stopped eating sweets ('I never thought a normal blood sugar level was something I would aspire to!'). She still met up with her friends, but for no more than two hours each time and a maximum of three times a week. She started meditating on a daily basis and taking frequent walks. Eliza: 'I felt like I was starting to live again. I became really good friends with myself. Memories started to flood back. Good memories of who I really was and what I liked doing. I was able to see the beauty in things again for the first time in years!'

After completing the second phase of recovery you can start thinking about going back to work again. However, it is best not to try working a full week immediately but to return to work bit by bit and under the watchful eye of your doctor or counsellor. Remember, reintegrating into your working environment is also part of the recovery from burnout. At first this will mean doing little more than going to your place of work, chatting with colleagues over a cup of coffee and getting used to the place again. This allows you to test what it feels like to be back in your old environment. After a few weeks you may be able to work a half day but only on tasks that are not too demanding. At this stage you don't have to shoulder any responsibility and are still getting used to being back in the saddle. From there it's a matter of slowly returning to your normal working schedule.

It is possible to make a complete recovery from a burnout. It requires a lot of help and support but with the right pace of recovery, supervision and a renewed self-confidence you can certainly get yourself back on your feet again. However, you need to be very careful not to push yourself over the edge and to listen to what your body needs.

## Hello body, are you okay?

We live in a time in which we do so much with our head that it is easy to forget we have a body, too. Our focus is very much on the brain, on logic and reason. We believe in the myth that you can achieve anything 'as long as you try hard enough.' And we like to do most of that trying with our brain. On the other hand, we expect our body to perform at its peak. What do you mean 'tired'? What do you mean 'not well'? Just pull up your socks and get on with it! We often rely on sheer willpower to push our body further than it wants to go. And if willpower doesn't work, we turn to caffeine, amphetamines and antidepressants.

It is not difficult to see yourself as a kind of walking brain. Often we are only really aware of our body when something goes wrong with it. Or when it deviates from the norm: too fat, too thin, too tall, too short, too flabby, too bony or too round in all the wrong places. Or when it doesn't run fast enough, jump high enough, dance well enough or isn't sexy enough. Compared with the perfect billboard bodies that serve as our role models, our own version is almost always a terrible disappointment.

So we try to forget our own body as much as we can and become less receptive to the signals telling us that we are tired or hungry or should try to slow things down a bit. This is what enables us to drive our body to the limit for years until it finally gives in. It's like getting into the habit of driving too fast and consistently ignoring all the speed limit signs on the motorway – sooner or later you will have to face the consequences. And for some people this means ending up with a body that just doesn't do what you want it to do.

For Eliza and Puck, simply becoming aware again of what was happening in their bodies was a fundamental part of their recovery. Puck: 'Meditation helped me to take notice of my body again, to realise that it speaks to me and that it is very important to treat it well. Sounds obvious, maybe, but it was a real eureka moment for me.'

Eliza has now gotten into the habit of asking herself, 'Hey body, are you okay?' A couple of times each day, she takes a moment to check in with her body and see how it's doing. Any time she detects signs of fatigue or restlessness, she adjusts her schedule accordingly, regardless of the plans she had for the day. For Eliza, her body comes before whatever obligations she might have. It is only when she is aware of what her body needs that she can keep stress at a safe distance.

Take a moment to ask yourself: how is my body feeling right now? What does it need? Are there signs of exhaustion, hunger or pain? What can you do to help it?

## After a burnout

I ask Marco to imagine that I have placed a large red button in front of him. As a thought experiment, I offer him a choice: if he pushes the button, the entire burnout episode will be erased from his life. It will simply never have happened. Will he push the button? Without a moment's hesitation he replies 'no'. 'In a way I'm happy I had a burnout, despite how weird that might sound. It has made me who I am now. I know more about myself and what drives me. And I also know how to deal with stress. It has taught me a few valuable lessons. Of course, it involved a lot of sacrifice, too. But that's life.'

When I ask Puck what she has learned from her burnout she says she has learned to listen to her body again. She pays better attention to her energy levels and as a result feels more in control of her own life. She advises anyone who suffers a burnout to choose what is best for them: 'Don't be afraid to say "No" when you have to. Not only because it will make life a lot easier for you, but also to prove to yourself that you have a choice. You are entitled to choose your own path if you wish, instead of following the same mad highway as everyone else.'

Burnout is not confined to the vulnerable or 'weak' among us. It can happen to anyone at any time. And even though it may

126

go against the notion that our lives ought to be 'perfect', we must remember that negative experiences are part of life, too. We are formed not only by our successes but also by our biggest challenges. Failure is part of the game and not something we need to be ashamed of. Puck, Eliza and Marco can all testify to that.

A burnout is:

- the 'last stop' on a person's stress journey and like an injury to your stress system;
- a state that forces you to take a complete break to recover from all the pent-up stress;
- often the result of years of pushing your body to the limit on the strength of willpower alone;
- usually characterised by many peaks and troughs, including disappointments and valuable insights;
- treatable given the right amount of rest and phased reintegration into your work.

# Intermezzo: relax!

## Picture this:

You are on a beach on a tropical island. It is a fabulous, sunny day and you are standing in the shade of a palm tree. Before you the water shimmers in the sunlight. A cool breeze keeps you from getting too warm. There is no one else around, apart from the seagull flying above your head.

You walk down to the shoreline. The beach seems to crackle under your feet. You step into the water and your feet disappear into the sand. The water is the perfect temperature. You take a deep breath and smell the salty air. You hear the wind rustling in the leaves of the palm tree. Everything else is all peace and quiet.

You have no worries on your mind. No one is demanding anything from you. There is nothing better you can spend your time on than just being right here, right now. And even if you wanted to be somewhere else, the boat won't be coming back to pick you up for another hour. No one can disturb you here. Embracing this hour of calm, you feel happy and relaxed.

You turn around and walk back to the shade of the palm tree. You sit down on the deck chair. On the table next to you is a coconut with a straw and a slice of watermelon sticking out of it. It tastes sweet and fruity. You lie back and close your eyes.

You wake up when you feel two hands massaging your neck and shoulders. You look around and see the face of someone you love. They tell you to close your eyes again and sit back and relax. You entrust yourself to their gentle hands. . .

How do you feel now? Probably a lot more relaxed than before you started to read this page. This is because there are certain things you can do to engender a sense of calm, such as imagining a relaxing situation as vividly as possible – a technique we call visualisation. We will address a few more of these techniques later on in the book.

But now – if you are feeling relaxed enough – let's carry on.

# 6
# WARNING!

Allow me to let you in on a little secret: dealing with stress is actually not all that complicated. Most of the things you can do to combat stress are fairly obvious: get enough sleep, eat healthily, exercise, get enough 'down time', reduce your workload and appointments and cancel all non-essential stuff.

You don't actually need me to tell you that. Research has shown that most people 'know' how to combat stress. Nevertheless, despite this knowledge, the majority of us fail to do what is required. This is very interesting from a psychological point of view: why are we so bad at looking after ourselves? With regard to stress, there are two main reasons: l) because what we want in the short term often contradicts our wishes for the long term; and 2) because we are very good at telling ourselves tall tales.

If you have ever smoked then you will know how easy it is to convince yourself that something that is bad for you is perfectly okay. Smoking is a good example of the kind of behaviour where the short-term goal (the instant satisfaction of pulling on a cigarette) directly contradicts the long-term one (living a long and healthy life). As a former 'occasional' smoker I can tell you this can be quite a pickle.

This presents us with a problem. After all, a conflict arises when a person is required to do something they don't agree with. This is known as cognitive dissonance: the problem that arises when your actions are not in line with your convictions. You can't really think one thing and do the opposite, hence the problem.

There are two ways of tackling this: the hard way and the easy way. The hard way is to discontinue the deviant behaviour, in this case smoking. This will certainly solve the problem, but it is difficult because smoking is extremely addictive. If this doesn't work (and for many smokers it never has!), you can choose the easy option: changing the way you *think* about your behaviour. If you are unable to change your behaviour, you then have to convince yourself that in your case this behaviour will not have a negative outcome. And this is where our amazing ability to sell ourselves bullshit comes to the fore. It is why smokers say things like: 'Smoking isn't bad for everyone. My aunt was a smoker and she lived to the age of 95' or 'I smoke every now and then but I can stop whenever I like.'

> In what ways could you take better care of yourself? Possible options are better eating habits, more sleep, regular exercise, drinking less alcohol, giving up smoking, etc. What things do you tell yourself to make something that is bad for you feel okay?

This is exactly what happens with stress, too. We often carry on being too busy for too long. Even though we would advise someone else in a similar position to slow down and take it easy, we rarely give ourselves the same advice. 'I'm taking a holiday in five weeks' time, so I'll be able to relax then', we tell ourselves, or 'The situation can't be helped. I'll just have to grin and bear it for the time being.' As long as you are able to convince yourself that everything will be better later, that you just need to hang in there, you will carry on as you are. Just like with smoking, you will only take action when things start to go wrong and by then it's usually too late. Once you reach the burnout stage, deciding to 'take it easy' doesn't help anymore. You then have no option but to shut up shop and start out on the long road to recovery.

Taking good care of yourself may not be the sexiest thing in the world, but it is absolutely essential. For one thing, you are one of the very few people you can rely on to provide the kind of self-care you need. The recipe for dealing with stress in a healthy manner is: recognising and acknowledging your own warning signs and then taking immediate action to alleviate the amount of pressure you are under. Of course, this sounds a lot easier than it actually is. You have to be able to do the following: look after your body, recognise your warning signs, take action when necessary and have an emergency plan ready for when it all goes horribly wrong.

## Essential maintenance

For a long time psychology was based on a clear division between body and mind. Psychologists focused almost exclusively on what went on between our ears. The body was not their responsibility; that was the domain of medical doctors, physiotherapists and gym instructors. Recently, however, there has been a growing realisation within psychology circles that the body and mind are deeply intertwined with each other, far more than anyone ever imagined.

The most recent insights have revealed that our mental health is determined to a large extent by our physical condition and there have been some remarkable discoveries in that regard. For example, we now know from studies that people make better decisions when they have an urge to pee (although no one seems to know exactly why). And scans have shown that our brain processes 'psychological' pain – such as the kind that arises out of social exclusion – the same way it does physical pain. In fact, you can even take an aspirin for that kind of pain!

The absence of a clear division between body and mind is also apparent in the case of stress. You suffer more from stress when you are feeling run down or are suffering from a flu. And if you have a bad night's sleep, everything is more stressful the next day. While you are more prone to stress when you are feeling poorly, the flip side is that you can combat it by looking after your body. It is now common knowledge that physical exercise (in addition to therapy) helps to alleviate depression. A healthy sleeping pattern also offers protection against all kinds of psychological disorders, and a healthy diet is known to reduce stress.

This is all good news. When you decide to do something about your stress levels it doesn't necessarily mean you have to turn your whole life upside down – quit your job, file for divorce, move to another country. Usually the first step is to take better care of your body, as this can lead to mental relief as well. Simply paying more attention to your physical well-being can make a big difference. The Canadian psychologist Jordan B. Peterson says this is the first thing he addresses with his clients: 'I have had many clients whose anxiety was reduced to subclinical levels merely because they started to sleep on a predictable schedule and eat breakfast.'

So you can reduce your stress levels by changing your lifestyle. In other words, combatting stress starts by carrying out essential maintenance on your body. Unfortunately, it is precisely this kind of maintenance that people suffering from stress tend to neglect. Taking good care of your body demands a lot of willpower – especially when you are very busy – but it almost always has an immediate and beneficial effect.

How's your diet? Do you eat enough (healthy food)? Most of us are familiar with the term 'hangry', a combination of hungry and angry. When you are hungry you can quickly become irritated by things that normally wouldn't bother you. But after you've had something to eat, the world is all bright and cheerful again. And what about the amount of coffee you drink? If you have to drink a litre of coffee every day just to stay awake, it's no wonder you are feeling stressed out.

The next topic we need to address is sleep. Getting enough sleep is very important for your body and vital to your brain. A lack of sleep has been linked to reduced reaction times and poor decision-making, more than a few glasses of alcohol can bring about, in fact. A regular sleep schedule – going to bed and waking up at more or less the same times – is essential when tackling stress. You don't have to stick to the schedule all of the time, but certainly for the most part. Even a sleeping pattern in which you go to bed and wake up at the same time for 80% of your week can be hugely beneficial. The regularity of your sleep schedule is as important as getting eight hours of sleep a day.

Finally, how do you spend your free time? Do you fill it with as much or as little activity as you can? Consider the difference between 'active' and 'passive' free time. Active free time is spent on things like hobbies, sport, friends and family. These are the hours in which you do things that are not related to your work but still provide you with energy and satisfaction. At the other end of the spectrum is passive free time: reading, watching TV, resting. Passive free time is actually the time you use to recover and build up your energy reserves again. Ideally you get to enjoy both active and passive free time – one to divert your attention from work and the other to regroup and recover. If your free time is almost always of the active kind, your life will be incredibly energetic but you will never have enough time to recover.

# Recognising your warning signs

| Physical | Cognitive |
| --- | --- |
| Tension (neck, shoulders) | Inability to concentrate |
| Unexplainable aches and pains | Seeing only the negative |
| Headache | Excessive worrying |
| Loss of libido | Memory problems |
| Frequent colds | Poorer decision skills |
| Rapid heartbeat | Anxious/racing mind |

| Emotional | Behaviour |
| --- | --- |
| Tense/irritable | Procrastination |
| Bad temper | Self-isolation |
| Depressed/general unhappiness | Eating more/less |
| Sense of loneliness/isolation | Sleeping more/less |
| Emotional instability | Using alcohol/drugs to relax |
| Feeling overwhelmed | Nervous tics (e.g., nail-biting) |

Stress does different things to different people. We all feel stress in different ways. It can take on many different forms. The symptoms vary greatly from person to person but usually remain the same for each individual. This means it is extremely important that you learn to identify your own warning signs, your own stress indicators.

On this page you saw a list of the most common warning signs. The list is by no means exhaustive and there are many more symptoms that people can experience as a result of stress. Not all of the warning signs on the list will be familiar to you (which is a good thing, believe me!) but your own specific symptoms are probably in there somewhere.

Stress can have physical, cognitive, emotional and behavioural symptoms. In other words, you can recognise stress from how you are thinking, from your emotions, how your body feels and how you act. You will often detect stress in several areas all at once.

For many, it is the physical symptoms of stress that are most familiar. Stress can cause headache and result in mysterious back or joint pain. It can lead to problems with digestion (diarrhoea or constipation), nausea and dizziness, a slower heartbeat or chest pain. A loss of libido can be the result of stress, too. And when you develop a chronically bad cold it can often be traced back to stress and a weakened immune system.[7]

Stress also has cognitive symptoms that are related to the way in which you think. We have already addressed a number of these, including poor decision-making and losing sight of the overall picture. Other cognitive symptoms are a lack of concentration, memory problems (e.g., not being able to remember certain words that you normally never have any trouble recalling), getting bogged down in the details, a muddled brain and focusing solely on the negative side of things.

We have already discussed some of the emotional symptoms of stress: a bad temper and an irritable and agitated disposition towards yourself and others. Other emotional warning signs include moodiness, the feeling that you are constantly playing catch-up and feelings of loneliness, anxiety and depression.

The behavioural symptoms of stress include not getting enough sleep (or sleeping too much), eating too little or too much and distancing yourself from others. Some people develop nervous tics like nail-biting and scratching, while others are prone to self-isolation. Alcohol and drug abuse or binging on Netflix to shut out the outside world can also be signs of excessive stress.

> Which warning signs on the list do you recognise? Which one usually comes first and which ones then follow? Think back to the last time you experienced excessive stress. Which warning signs did you notice at the time?

My apologies if this section of the book comes across as anything but cheerful, what with all its unpleasant stress symptoms. You were probably hoping that reading this book would be an enjoyable experience, too. However, all going well, you should have a much better idea now of your own warning signs and know what to watch out for in the future when you are under pressure. And that is essential if you want to be able to take action on time.

## Taking action

The next step is knowing how and when to take action. This requires you to take a critical look at how much you have on your plate and to jettison some of your workload where possible. Easier said than done, of course. It takes a lot of time and courage to intervene when necessary. It requires you to admit to yourself and to those around you that you are vulnerable. Sometimes it will involve disappointing others, too. There are people who depend on you and they will suffer when you have to let them down. And then there's the stigma attached to saying 'no'. You may have an in-built expectation that you should be able to do everything that is asked of you. After all, your friends and colleagues are able to keep going, so why can't you?

Even when you afford yourself a bit more breathing space, it can be difficult to decide which things to remove from your workload. Which things can you cancel? What can be postponed? What can you stop doing altogether? Everything may feel equally important. If you have difficulty deciding what should be given priority, the exercises in the next chapter will help.

There is an art to cancelling appointments without coming across as unreliable or rubbing people up the wrong way. One in which your most important tools of timing and communication must come into play. The sooner you notice your diary becoming full, the easier it is to cancel or postpone an appointment. Cancelling at the last moment is a sure source of irritation. How you go about cancelling an appointment is therefore very important. You need to be able to explain your reasons without making it look like you're fishing for sympathy.

Studies have shown that if you use the word 'because' when asking someone something, people are more likely to go along with you. This principle can also be applied when cancelling an appointment: 'I've just had a look at my schedule and it looks like I'm going to have to postpone our meeting on Tuesday until a later date because I have to finish a lot of work for another project first. I'd prefer to pick another date when I have more time. Is that okay with you?'

In his book *12 Rules for Life* Jordan B. Peterson describes a phenomenon that continues to puzzle doctors everywhere. A large percentage of the patients for whom they issue prescriptions regularly fail to complete the course of medication as instructed and this often leads to more problems for the patient. This applies not only to prescriptions like antibiotics for a throat infection but also to medication that prevents the body from rejecting an organ after a transplant.

You would think that someone who is prescribed medication after undergoing a kidney transplant would be pretty careful about taking their pills. But many patients fail to continue taking their medication even when this may lead to life-threatening situations. However, if someone is responsible for making sure that their child, an older family member or even a pet takes their medication, then they usually do exactly that. Peterson's conclusion is that we tend to take much better care of other people, and even our pets, than we do of ourselves. His advice is to look after ourselves the same way we would look after someone else.

The tips in this chapter are not all that complicated and you may even have come up with some of them yourself in the past. In fact, chances are that you have offered this kind of advice to others when they came to you complaining of stress. We find it much easier to allow other people to take a backseat every now and then than we do ourselves.

That's why I think it is often a good idea to ask yourself what you would advise another person to do if they were in a similar position and then apply that advice to your own situation.

No matter how difficult it may be to make changes to your workload or the way you fill your day, the alternative – doing nothing – is a lot worse. As we have already seen, sticking rigidly to your schedule because you feel you must is a surefire way of ending up with a burnout. If you want to be able to function effectively in the long term, you have to take things easier in the short term. You may even find that others are more willing to accept this than you are. Your boss at work or those near and dear to you often display a lot of understanding for your situation simply because your well-being is more important to them than your ability to live up to their expectations. They are often far better at seeing how important it is that you look after yourself.

When you are ill and cannot work you just have to accept the fact that you will be temporarily out of action. The same goes for excessive stress. We now know that stress can make you as ill as a virus can and that stress can have major implications for your health in the long term. Taking action before things get out of hand is not only advisable but often also essential. And while this may not make me very popular among employers, as far as I'm concerned you should be allowed to call in sick when you are suffering from stress so that you can prevent the situation from getting worse. I believe you have every right to do whatever is required. Taking care of yourself is not a luxury but a responsibility, towards yourself and towards others, too.

## Contingency plan

Every company, indeed every government has one lying in a safe: a plan for when everything goes terribly wrong. It's called a contingency plan: a protocol for when the shit hits the fan. It describes the steps that must be taken when the unthinkable happens. It ensures there is a well thought-out plan in place that can be used in a worst-case scenario. The last thing you want in a crisis is to have everyone walking around scratching their heads and wondering, 'What do we do now?'

This kind of plan often requires the declaration of a state of emergency in which extraordinary measures may be taken to prevent everything from going completely down the swanny. Sometimes draconian measures are required to get yourself out of trouble.

It is a good idea to have a contingency plan in place for when your stress levels go sky-high. And it is always smart to formulate the plan before you are overcome by stress because often the first thing that disappears in a stressful situation is your ability to think clearly and make good decisions.

What should your contingency plan contain? Firstly, a list of practical steps you can take to immediately relieve some of the pressure. If your warning signs start to flash, you will know exactly what to do. These steps must be as clear as possible. Which things should you cancel straight away? How can you make sure you continue to get enough sleep? Can you alter your diet to ensure that you are eating well? What can you do to divert your attention from your head to your body? How can you create some (passive) relaxation time? Who can you turn to for help and support?

My own contingency plan contains the following steps:

- Open my diary and see what I can skip or cancel.
- Switch from drinking gallons of coffee to cups of herbal tea.
- Cut out all sugar; consume more proteins and less carbohydrates.
- Walk to the train station or to work instead of driving or cycling. (This gives me more time to think and I feel under less pressure to hurry).
- Immediately free up two evenings in the week just to plonk myself on the sofa. (If I already had other appointments, tough luck. This is more important!).
- Set my telephone to 'do not disturb' or flight mode.
- Switch to working on a different laptop that has no access to e-mail or social media.
- Set an alarm to go off at random intervals throughout the day and do a breathing exercise when the alarm sounds.

What would your contingency plan look like?

Draw up your own contingency plan. In it describe the practical steps you will take when your stress levels go up. Use a metaphor that suits your situation. Provide your plan with a visual element (a flow chart, mind map, symbols or illustrations instead of just text) because your brain just loves visual information.

# Warning!

The steps in this chapter can help you to lower your stress levels. Use them each time you are faced with a stressful situation. You will then know what to do when the pressure becomes too much and you need to adjust your workload. But there are also strategies for preventing stress from arising in the first place and we will address these in the following chapters.

You can deal with stress by:

- giving your body what it needs: proper maintenance with regard to sleep, diet, rest and exercise;
- taking care of yourself as if you were someone else who has entrusted their care to you;
- learning to recognise your warning signs at an early stage;
- taking action by adjusting your workload and cancelling appointments;
- when necessary, executing a contingency plan with measures designed to combat stress.

# 7
# PEACE OF MIND

Razor-sharp knives, red-hot frying pans and lots of people working in a confined space – the kitchen in a restaurant can be a very dangerous place. When the restaurant is fully booked it becomes a fast-moving production machine with a single task: to cook and serve one perfect dish after another at a blistering pace. It requires a lot of preparation. Everything in the kitchen is designed to prevent chaos. The only way you can serve hundreds of dishes within a short period of time is when everything is exactly where it is supposed to be (*mise-en-place*, as the French say). You have to be able to find what you need without thinking and preferably even without looking. Only when you can trust that everything is within hand's reach can you produce an endless stream of culinary delights.

If the thing you need is not where it's supposed to be, you're in trouble. You lose your focus, have to stop what you were doing and try to find the goddam meat thermometer or whatever it was you needed. In the meantime, your colleagues start glaring at you for disturbing their concentration, while the orders continue to come in thick and fast. It takes you 15 minutes to get back into the flow again. But not before the head chef reads you the riot act for stepping out of line.

I have never worked (or cooked) as efficiently as I did during my brief career as a chef. Today my own kitchen is a nightmare: never enough space and always too much stuff getting in the way. I can never find that one essential thing when I need it the most. Nothing is ever where it is supposed to be, there is always a big pile of dirty dishes in the sink and when I have to stretch to get something from a top shelf I usually end up knocking over all the other stuff up there as well. It's the kind of kitchen where you have to be very careful about opening a cupboard if you don't want to be buried under an avalanche of rice and spaghetti. Preparing even the simplest pasta dish is a major challenge because I have to spend half an hour cleaning up first. No wonder I prefer eating out to eating in.

What applies to the kitchen also applies to your head. A head that is full to bursting – like my kitchen – leads to turmoil and delay. Everything becomes more difficult when your mind is overloaded. The simplest tasks take far more time and energy than they should. In the absence of a system all you are left with is chaos.

The good news is that you can set your head up to operate like the kitchen in a restaurant. This requires you to find a system that works for you, which demands some effort, of course, but it will make your work a lot easier and enable you to perform even under immense pressure. Running your head like you would a kitchen is a good way of avoiding high levels of stress.

What would it be like if you were able to do everything you normally do with a lot less stress and agitation? Imagine you were able to rid your mind of all unnecessary worry and concentrate on the stuff that really matters. What would it be like if you could always see the bigger picture and feel like you are able to get everything done on time? What would you give to be able to live like that? In this chapter we will explore a number of tricks and techniques that will help you to tick those boxes, achieve stress-free productivity and bring a little more calm into your life.

## Make time for yourself

Here's a delicate question: how much time do you spend scrolling through social media every day? And I don't mean those moments on your timeline that provide you with entertainment and relaxation. I mean the time you're wasting. The time you spend on apps that don't give you anything in return on a personal or professional level.

A few years ago I attended a lecture during which computer scientist Cal Newport posed this very question. I immediately tried to work out my own answer. At first I was pretty confident that I used my time fairly efficiently. However, it turned out that I had far more time wasters during my day than I had anticipated. And the worst offender? Facebook. It appeared I was spending an awful lot of time scrolling through my timeline until an interesting bit of content popped up on the screen.

I discovered that I spent up to 20 minutes each day scrolling through Facebook. At first I figured this was reasonable enough, until I started to crunch the numbers. Twenty minutes a day adds up to around two hours a week, which is one whole working day per month and two full working weeks per year. In the ten years that I have been active on this particular platform it has taken up a total of two and a half months of my time. Ten whole weeks that would have been better spent with my family and friends, learning a new language or taking a trip around the world. Instead, all that time was spent trawling through other people's photos and reacting to posts from people I barely even know.

> What are your worst time wasters? Make a list of your time wasters and calculate the amount of time you spend on each one per week, per month and per year. Are the figures acceptable to you or would you prefer to have spent your time on something else?

If you want to find more peace of mind, some of these notorious time wasters will simply have to go. Many of the platforms and services that we use on a daily basis – Facebook, Snapchat, Instagram, WhatsApp – make their money by exploiting our engagement on their digital playgrounds. They employ armies of psychologists with a formidable arsenal of tricks at their disposal to make sure you stay addicted and tuned in. All available means are used: social pressure ('If you quit Facebook, Rita and Joe will really miss you!'), our sensitivity to FOMO ('We haven't seen you the past few days, you don't know what you're missing!') and other forms of aggressive marketing. In the meantime, your personal details are being sold to the highest bidder. To quote a widely-used phrase on the subject of the internet, 'If you're not paying for it, you're the product.'

Don't get me wrong, I'm not trying to tell you that you need to be productive every single minute of the day. In fact, relaxation (and even boredom!) is essential if you want to be able to come up with new ideas. It's also essential to your mental well-being. But can you really call the time you spend on social media and its constant stream of information and stimuli 'relaxing'? And does it offer you enough in return for all the precious time it claims?

I believe we need to think long and hard about which things are worth spending our time on and which ones aren't. Remember, if you don't choose where to focus your attention, someone else will make that decision for you.

Your time and attention are among the most precious commodities you possess, so make them count.

## An empty mind

Memorise these numbers: 6 – 9 – 8 – 3 – 1 – 9 – 4. Done? Okay. Now cover them with a piece of paper.

Have you ever tried to remember something for a whole day? It's very hard work for your brain. This is because there is a limit to the amount of stuff we can remember. We can recall around seven separate pieces of information without too much trouble after we have repeated them back to ourselves often enough. (Can you still recall the numbers I asked you to memorise?). Storing more than seven things in your memory at a time is difficult, particularly when you already have several open cognitive loops on the go reminding you to buy cat food and to send Diana an e-mail about your upcoming project.

The human brain is not great at storing stuff. It is actually designed to remember things that are important and to forget the rest. When the working memory in your brain becomes overcrowded with information the result is usually chaos. Picture a desk piling up with a constant stream of new files until there are so many it is impossible to continue working. Similarly, when your brain is under too much mental pressure it becomes difficult to concentrate and think clearly. If you want a more relaxed brain, you need to keep your workload to a minimum and close as many of those cognitive loops as possible.

When you explore the art of achieving an empty mind it is impossible to ignore the work of the consultant David Allen and his GTD (Getting Things Done) method. According to Allen, our mind is designed to perform specific functions: generate ideas, formulate plans and solve problems – in short, to be creative. Our brain is not as good at doing the other things it is often asked to do, like multitasking or storing large amounts of information in our memory. To quote Allen directly, 'the mind is for having ideas, not storing them.'

According to Allen, achieving an empty mind is really quite simple. All you have to do is stop trying to store stuff in your head and store it somewhere else instead. And how do you do that? By creating a storage system for things you want to remember, for example in a task manager, an email to yourself or an old-fashioned notebook. This allows you to immediately store each incoming piece of information instead of burdening your brain with the task. Allen's GTD method can be applied to everything you need to remember: contact details, shopping lists, arguments, new ideas, restaurant recommendations, vague plans and anything else you might need to act upon at a later date. All these bits and pieces of information – regardless of how important they are – represent the extraneous things in your metaphorical kitchen that often make cooking dinner a real pain in the ass.

At the start or end of your day (or another time that suits you better) take half an hour to study the list you have made of all your bits and pieces of information. For each item, decide whether it is something you need to do immediately or not. If it is a vague idea or something you are not sure about, add it to your 'to-maybe-do' list. For things you think need to be acted upon there are two options, based on Allen's two-minute-rule: if it can be done in two minutes or less (a simple e-mail/app), do it immediately. You won't save any time by postponing it until later, so best to tackle it straightaway. For all other tasks: make sure you list them clearly and schedule them for a time that suits you.

Imagine you are out cycling and pedalling along on automatic pilot. Suddenly you remember that you have been waiting for an important e-mail from a client. You decide it is high time you sent them a reminder. You could get off your bike and send the mail from your phone but you prefer not to send e-mails that way. You could also try to store the mail you want to send in your brain but that would cost too much mental energy. Another option is to jot the e-mail down in a notebook (or record it on your phone). Doing that will allow you to remove the e-mail from your mind. The following day you see the note 'reminder mail to client X' on your list and you make a plan to write and send it at your earliest convenience.

Jotting down a thought means you can immediately close an open cognitive loop and eliminate the need to remember that thought. This allows you to use the scarce capacity in your brain for more important stuff: taking in everything around you, making space for flashes of inspiration and paying attention to the road as you cycle along. The less you have to remember, the more attention you can pay to other things.

(Can you still recall the numbers you memorised at the beginning of this section? If you can, well done, you've just won yourself a cuddly toy. But were you able to pay close attention to what you were reading at the same time?)

In the coming week, try using David Allen's method. Devise a system for storing your ideas, cognitive loops and flashes of inspiration. You could use your smartphone (the notes app, an e-mail to yourself) or a simple notebook that you keep on your person at all times. You could also try an app called Braintoss which can send a voice message directly to your mailbox. Train yourself to write things down and remove them from your mind. Each day, pick a moment that suits you and spend half an hour turning all the bits and pieces of information you have gathered into actual tasks. Voilà, you've just created an empty mind!

## Goals

We humans are very goal-oriented beings. Arriving on time at work can be a goal, as can making an aubergine bake for tonight's dinner. These goals demand different kinds of action, such as setting your alarm clock and leaving the house on time or going to the supermarket to buy aubergines. Although we don't often realise it, we spend much of our day setting goals for ourselves and attempting to achieve them. If we are unable to set goals, however, it becomes very difficult to take action and get things done.

The examples above don't really require you to put your goals down in writing, but it is important to do so in the case of bigger goals. For those goals, the clearer you can describe what you are trying to achieve, the better you will be able to focus your efforts and the greater your chances of success.

Imagine you want to lose some weight. This is not a clear enough goal in itself because there is no way of knowing when you have reached your goal. How much weight, precisely, and within which time frame? What would be a satisfactory result? If your goal is merely 'to lose some weight', you will never know when you are done. All you will know is that you're not quite there yet and that can be disastrous for your motivation. You will only find the drive required to make a real effort when you have a clear and concise goal: 'I want to lose five kilos in three months.'

Most of us are familiar with the tools that can be used to set goals. There are models that are used in every team, every training course and every organisation. In fact, they are so well known that when I start talking to my students about setting goals they often start rolling their eyes and sighing heavily; they've been hearing the same old story since they were in secondary school.

According to the most popular of these models – the SMART model – a goal has to meet the following requirements: the outcome must be formulated as *Specifically* as possible, the goal must be *Measurable* in order to track progress, the result must be *Acceptable* to you and to others, it must be *Realistic* and it must be *Time-bound* (there has to be a deadline). This enables you to set goals that are precise and detailed and that dictate the action you need to take to achieve them. For example, 'For the next two weeks I am going to do a five-minute breathing exercise in the morning and in the evening.'

There is another important aspect of setting goals that is crucial to motivation: the distinction between what I call 'performance goals' and 'development goals'.

A performance goal refers to something you want to make happen, a specific kind of result. An example: 'In two months' time I want to have found a new job that I'm happy doing.' A performance goal like this specifies the situation you would prefer to be in. The problem with performance goals, however, is that your performance also depends on what others do and other external factors. For instance, there has to be a vacancy somewhere for the kind of job you are looking for and your prospective employer also has to decide to hire you for the position. When you are more inclined to set performance goals you are often at the mercy of factors beyond your own control. This can quickly lead to disappointment and higher levels of stress if you fail to achieve your goal despite your best efforts.

To avoid this outcome, it is often better to set yourself a development goal instead. A development goal does not describe the desired outcome, but rather specifies what you need to do to achieve it. In the case of a development goal, you are not dependent on others or on external factors. The focus is not on what you want from the world but on what you intend to do to achieve your goal. When applied to the example above we could say, 'This month I am going to send at least five job applications to firms where I would like to work.'

Using the guidelines above, set yourself a development goal for dealing with stress. For example, this week I will check my e-mail no more than twice a day – once in the morning and once in the evening.

## Priorities

Whenever I give training on stress-free working, the following is the part I look forward to most because it gives me the chance to play the magician for a few minutes.[8] I take a big pickle jar from my bag, put it on my desk and announce to the group: 'This empty jar represents the amount of time you can spend on stuff in a week. The jar is pretty big but it is not infinitely big – after all, there are only so many hours in a week.' Then I produce a bag of ping-pong balls and tip them into the jar until it is full to the brim. I explain that the balls represent your priorities – your most important activities, the things that are important in terms of achieving your goals. If you are a care worker, this would probably be caring for your patients, while for a scientist it would be doing research. Those activities could also involve the things outside your work that are most valuable to you; spending time with your family and friends or working on your own personal development, for example.

You can't squeeze any more ping-pong balls into the jar, but does that mean it's full? No, pipes up a smart trainee in the group. And she's right – there is still room between the ping-pong balls for a handful of marbles. These represent the less important tasks that are also unavoidable, such as meetings with your colleagues or grading papers.

So is the jar now full? No. With a theatrical flourish I pour a bag of sand over the ping-pong balls and marbles. The sand represents those things that are unimportant to you but that you are still required to do. Things like administrative tasks at work or getting to and from your place of work. And just when everyone thinks the jar is definitely full, I add in a glass of water. The water stands for the things that are unimportant and that you do not have to do, but that you still find yourself doing anyway – reading newsletters that contain no useful information or checking Instagram (again) to see if anything interesting has been posted since the last time you looked.

Okay, playing the magician with a jar of mud-covered ping-pong balls is all great fun, but what's the point? The point is that many people fill their jar the wrong way around. They start with the sand and hope there will be enough room left at the end for their ping-pong balls and a few marbles. The result is usually bitter disappointment. Trying to squeeze a ping-pong ball into a jar that's already full of muddy marbles is not much fun and you will only end up making a terrible mess.

Your busy life, both personally and professionally speaking, means there will always be enough sand and water waiting to fill your jar. If you don't make conscious choices regarding how to fill your time, you will never finish your most important tasks. And this is where prioritising comes in. It's such a waste when you fill your jar first with sand only to realise that you have forgotten to leave room for your ping-pong balls. You need to focus on the important stuff first before turning your attention to more trivial matters.

> What are your ping-pong balls? What are your marbles? And what things represent your sand and water? How do you fill your own jar?

- Ping-pong balls = the really important stuff that you do in your work and personal life (= your priorities!).
- Marbles = unavoidable but not necessarily important things.
- Sand = stuff that is unimportant to you but that you still have to do.
- Water = things that are neither important nor unavoidable.

Another way of identifying your priorities is by conducting the following thought experiment. Imagine if the government decided – for improbable yet plausible reasons – to abolish

Tuesdays. No one likes Tuesdays anyway and there are sound economic reasons for scrapping the day altogether. It means you are forced to rethink how you fill your week because you have to find the time somewhere for the important stuff. Which things would you make time for and which things would fail to make the cut? And there is an extra catch: you have to do this without cutting back on your sleep or free time! The activities that you retain in your new, shorter week are obviously those that are most important to you. And the things that you no longer have time for are found to be of less importance.

Now turn the thought experiment on its head. Imagine that instead of scrapping a day the government decides to add an extra day between Wednesday and Thursday called 'Lumberday'. What would you use this day for? Which plans would you allocate more time to and which things would you finally get around to doing? Your answers will reveal those things that are important to you but that you never have the time to do.

There are many things we could say about the abilities of the various presidents of the United States, but one thing they all knew how to do is delegate. Faced with the Cold War, the Space Race and the war in Korea, Dwight Eisenhower (US president from 1953 to 1961) had more than enough on his plate. As a result, you never saw him worrying about how to formulate the perfect speech or what he should get the staff at the White House for Christmas. Rumour has it he developed a tool he could use to identify the things that should be given high priority and the things he could delegate to others or even ignore. This tool eventually became known as the Eisenhower Matrix.

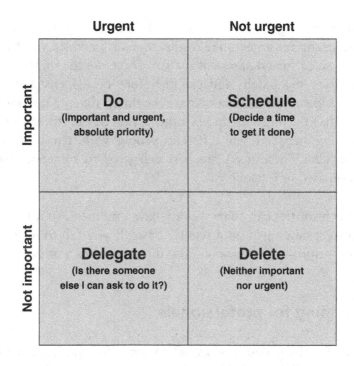

The matrix works as follows. When a request or task lands on your desk you ask two questions: 'Is it important?' and 'Is it urgent?' 'Important' here means: significant in terms of achieving your own goals or the goals attached to your work. 'Urgent' means something that has to be done quickly or is subject to a tight deadline. Depending on the answer to these questions, the task will fall under one of the four categories in the matrix and you will know exactly how to respond.

If something is both important and urgent – for example, filing your tax returns just before the deadline – do it immediately. It's an absolute priority. If something is important but not urgent – thinking about your career in the long term, for instance, or writing a business plan – add it to your schedule.

The lower right-hand box is for the things that are neither important nor urgent, like reading e-mails in which you have been cc'ed for no apparent reason. These are the things that are 'Not my patch' and can therefore be dispensed with. In the lower left-hand corner are the things that are unimportant to you but nonetheless urgent, like having to set up a meeting between ten different people with ten different schedules. These tasks are best delegated to someone else, automated or outsourced.

Your priorities can change at any given moment, so it is useful to review them on a regular basis. If you fail to identify your priorities, pretty soon everything becomes a priority.

## Planning for professionals

Another thing that is essential to stress-free productivity is planning. Planning brings order to chaos. A good plan is the difference between 'plain sailing' and 'total madness'. Planning is the unsung hero of your hectic life, and while having good planning skills may be neither glamorous nor sexy, being able to plan well can be a real life-saver at times. So, long live the plan!

Isn't planning simply a matter of fitting the things you have to do into your working schedule? Partly, yes, but there's more to it than that. Efficient planning ensures you have enough time to address crucial matters without having to wonder where you are going to find the time. It creates a sense of calm, because as long as you have a good plan you will never have to worry about things not being done on time. It provides you with a clear overall picture, even in the face of a heavy workload. If your planning is smooth, you can park many of your concerns regarding deadlines and results in your (digital) diary so that you can free up your mind for other things, such as reflecting on your work or simply enjoying the present moment.

When I began writing this book I quickly noticed that I was spending a large portion of my week making appointments, filling in meeting planners (I hate meeting planners and their multifarious possibilities!) and scheduling interviews. I spent so much time mailing and calling people that I barely found the time to put pen to paper. Pretty soon I realised I couldn't go on like this.

As an experiment I decided to hire Selma. It turns out there are people who like organising things and Selma is one of them. She was crazy enough to accept my offer and so I hired her as my personal assistant for a few hours a week. It wasn't long before Selma had straightened out my diary and appointments (and presented me with a large jar and three bags of ping-pong balls, marbles and sand to use in my training programme). In a word, Selma is AWESOME. She is also partly responsible for bringing this book to fruition. I would recommend a Selma to anyone any day.

I thought I was fairly good at planning stuff until Selma introduced me to the art of planning for professionals. She got me to substitute my paper diary for a digital one – a change I had always been reluctant to make. It turned out to be an inspired move. Suddenly I not only had all my appointments displayed neatly before me but in different colours, too, and with lots of other useful information as well. It was all so ... organised! She instructed me to draw up my schedule as if I was doing it for someone else. This cleared up most of the confusion in my diary. In one fell swoop my good old Opel Corsa of a diary had become a supersonic Ferrari.

Not everyone can afford a Selma, of course. But don't worry, there's plenty you can do yourself, too. The tips below come from years of experience with planning, the training I received from my coach, Aik Kramer, and the final touch courtesy of Selma. They will help you to be prepared for any eventuality, whether you are a student getting ready for an exam or are a parent trying to combine family life with a demanding job.

The aim of efficient planning is to create a clear overall picture and a clear mind. That's why it is useful to keep a digital or paper record of everything so that your brain does not have to store vast amounts of information. Make sure your schedule offers you a clear picture of everything you are doing so that you can immediately see what you have to do and when. And use different colours to mark different projects or categories, so that everything is easy to read.

A schedule is never static. It is a living organism and for it to function properly you must monitor it on a daily basis and make whatever adjustments are necessary. Take ten minutes each day (or whatever time you can spare) to review your daily schedule. For each planned task, ask yourself: is this the best approach and is the task still necessary? Life rarely dovetails seamlessly with your plans, so you often have to adjust them to suit events in your life. Your plans will be regularly disrupted by stuff that comes along unexpectedly. But that doesn't have to be a problem or mean that you have to throw all your plans out the window. You just need to adjust. After all, you wouldn't dump your Ferrari on the side of the road just because of a warning light on your dashboard, would you?

I recently heard one of my students say, 'All my planning is going fine. It's just a pity I can't find any room in my diary for spontaneous stuff!' If that's the case, there's something seriously wrong with your planning. The aim of efficient planning is to make you more flexible, not less. It should also make you more motivated and less stressed. If that is not the case then you have too much on your plate or have failed to clearly identify your priorities (Do I have to do this now?). Having so many plans that it stresses you out is not a smart strategy. Remember, life is a marathon not a sprint, so make sure that you schedule enough free time for yourself and always keep some time free in your work diary as well. You will only be able to keep going in the long term when your planning contains space for doing literally nothing as well as for doing the things you enjoy. Plan your day in the ideal way so that you can do what is required of you but in a manner that is both relaxed and agreeable.

A list of deadlines is not a plan. Neither is it good for your motivation. You need to draw up a schedule for when you will work on individual tasks and not just for when they have to be completed. Decide when you are going to work on a particular task and allot it the required time in your diary. If it is a time-consuming task, block a few hours for it – it often takes at least an hour to build up some speed on a big job. Do this and when you look at your diary you will be able to say 'All is going according to plan and I have enough time to work on everything' instead of 'Shit, I have to get all of this done before Friday!'

It can also be useful to work with buffers, given that your plans will always be subject to sudden and unexpected change. Buffers are blocks of time that you schedule for a particular project but that also contain enough room for manoeuvre. They represent 'extra' time for when things go wrong in your planning (which will be a regular occurrence). Buffers make you flexible. For instance, if I have to correct my students' work and I need around ten hours to do so, I will block twelve hours in my diary. This immediately relieves any potential pressure. And in the exceptional case that everything goes precisely according to plan, I will have a few extra hours for myself. A nice bonus!

If you have to travel for your work, it is advisable to schedule some 'non-productive' time before and after appointments and to include your travel time in your planning. Ideally, you should plan for just a little more time than you will actually need. Adding enough travel time to your planning can make a huge difference in terms of stress. The same applies to the more or less unproductive time you spend waiting between appointments. Add that time to your planning, too, and don't fill it with other things to do. Believe me, the guy who spends his time talking loudly on the phone while travelling back to the office on a train full to bursting with commuters doesn't have many fans. For good measure you should also add an extra 10% for possible delays when travelling to and from work, just to be on the safe (and sane) side.

If you use these tips in a consistent manner, it will make a real difference to your stress levels. It may all sound a little neurotic, but you will be repaid handsomely in terms of peace of mind. Selma and I are prepared to stick our necks out on that one for you.

---

The most important rules of thumb for efficient planning:

- Create a plan for all your activities and mark them using different colours. An efficient plan is one that facilitates a clear overall picture and a clear mind;
- Life does not adapt to fit your schedule, so you will have to adapt your plans to fit your life. Take some time each day (or once or twice a week) to update your schedule;
- Plan ahead not just to meet your deadlines but also to schedule a specific time for starting a new project;
- Make sure you have enough free time in your schedule (especially when you are very busy);
- Create buffers for when you are working on large projects so that you can be flexible and won't panic when things don't go according to plan.

# Pulling rank on e-mail

E-mail. Where would we be without it? We send each other billions of e-mails every day. In a previous chapter we have already addressed the negative consequences of our addiction to e-mail: greatly reduced working time, fragmented attention and a veritable bombardment of information. And things can be even worse when you are what is known as an inbox zero person: someone who can only relax when their inbox is completely empty.

E-mail is disastrous for your concentration and can cost you enormous amounts of time and energy if you're not careful. Before you know it, your mailbox can become a kind of to-do list to which other people have access; an assembly point where others can dump jobs for you to do, often without them even realising it. You have no control over what ends up in your mailbox, so e-mail can very easily become a constant source of stress. Thankfully there are a number of strategies you can employ to avoid this scenario.

There's no harm in playing hard to get every now and then. This applies not only to your dating strategy but also to e-mail. Most people don't actually expect you to reply to their e-mail within an hour. You can be sure they'll call you on the phone if it's really urgent. Close your e-mail programme when you're not using it and turn off those silly notifications that flash on your screen when there's a new message in your inbox. E-mail was never designed to be a medium that requires you to reply immediately to the person on the other end. In my experience it's rarely a problem if you wait until the following day before sending a reply. This can even have an added advantage: problems often have the tendency to get solved in some other way when you don't respond straight away. And remember, back when most of our mail came through the letterbox no one ever stood waiting patiently by the door for the postman to arrive.

Of course, your job may actually require you to reply immediately to questions from customers or colleagues. In that case you do need to check your inbox on a regular basis. However, it can be helpful to draw a distinction between when your mailbox has to be left open and when you can leave it closed. If possible, make sure you have at least some time during the day in which you don't find yourself reacting instinctively to whatever lands in your inbox.

Here's another thing I wish I'd known ten years ago: you are not obliged to reply to an e-mail simply because someone has sent it to you. In fact, it is often a good idea to ignore unsolicited e-mails, as any reply you send will invariably invite yet another bloody reply. Ask yourself: is this e-mail really relevant to me? Is it important to my goals? If the answer is no, you can delete the e-mail without replying to it. It may not be polite, but that's not always a bad thing. Another trick is to distinguish between e-mails that require more of your time and attention (schedule these for when you have enough time) and e-mails that can be dealt with quickly. You can block a half hour at the start or end of your day to process as many of the latter category as possible.

Reading this chapter may help change the way you use e-mail. Unfortunately, that does not necessarily apply to the people who e-mail you. And that's why it is an excellent idea to give this book to others as a gift. . . All joking aside, the only other real option is expectation management: making clear to others how you wish to use e-mail. Tell those around you that you regard e-mail as a medium for sending messages that do not require an immediate response. If they need to contact you urgently, they should use the telephone and you can even reassure them that you will respond to all contact via the telephone within two hours.

Using your e-mail signature and the autoreply function can also help. You can add a remark at the bottom of your e-mails along the lines of: 'For both our sakes I endeavour to restrict my replies to all e-mails to one or two lines.' Your autoreply can make it clear to others that you only ever read your e-mails at the start and end of your working day and that for urgent matters you may be contacted by telephone. These tips can help to make everything crystal clear for everyone involved.

> Leave one e-mail unanswered each day. Save your reply for later, send an e-mail saying that you will reply in more detail when you have the time or just ignore the e-mail altogether. Why? To remind yourself that it is your choice whether to reply to an e-mail or not.

## The power of habit

It is no secret that gyms and fitness centres earn the lion's share of their income immediately after 31 December when people are bursting with New Year's resolutions and motivation. Many sign up for an annual subscription in the firm belief that they will make full use of it. However, most of these new subscribers spend no more than a few weeks on the treadmill before failing to show up again for the rest of the year.

Generally speaking, New Year's resolutions rarely last very long. This is because changing your behaviour is actually extremely difficult. Almost everyone has a habit or two they would like to change: eat less sugar, get more exercise, quit smoking, drink more water or cut down on alcohol. Changing your behaviour may sound simple but it demands a tremendous amount of willpower. And I'm speaking from experience. Each year, without fail, I manage to allow a steadfast New Year's resolution fall by the wayside only a few weeks into January.

There are people who are able to jump out of bed every morning before 7 a.m. full of energy and ready to face the day. I have great (but sometimes grudging) admiration for these people, mainly because I love sleeping in. If I don't have any pressing engagements in the morning, it often requires a massive effort to crawl out from under the covers. When I forget to set my alarm – or sleep straight through it, an all-too-common occurrence – I often wake up at 10 a.m. in a state of complete panic. And if I do set an alarm, I am usually very good at convincing myself that five more minutes won't do any harm. I am always able to come up with excellent arguments for snoozing just a little bit longer. Eventually, when I do get up, I may feel well rested but this will invariably be accompanied by a heavy sense of guilt at having let a significant portion of my day slip though my fingers again.

As a kind of test I decided to make a point of getting up early while writing this book. Setting the goal was the easy part – rise at 7 a.m. each morning during the week – and for the first week it went very well. I was actually quite proud of myself. In fact, I even became a bit too confident and considered setting the alarm for 6 a.m. so that I could add an extra hour on to my day. In the second week, however, and despite my best intentions, I only managed to get up at 7 a.m. on three occasions. I soon discovered that getting up early was a lot easier when you went to bed early as well – who would have thought? But the presentation I gave on Tuesday evening ran late and on Thursday I decided to catch a late movie with my friends. By the third week I was barely managing to get up on time at all. Yet another failed attempt at self-improvement.

I imagine you have probably had similar experiences yourself. If that's the case, don't worry, you are not alone. Finding the motivation to change your behaviour may appear relatively easy at first but it gets harder and harder as time goes by. This applies both to the things you would like to do more of (exercise, meditation) and the things you would like to cut back on (checking your e-mail, smoking).

It all has to do with willpower. You have to make a deliberate decision each time you want to exhibit a certain kind of behaviour. Going to the gym or declining a slice of cake is easy enough the first time around. You are also rewarded with the nice feeling that comes with achieving a goal: you feel like a superhero and it wasn't even all that difficult to do what was required of you. However, as time goes by the sense of euphoria wanes and the need for more willpower increases. The reward you experience also becomes less significant the more 'normal' it becomes, while the discipline required becomes greater. As the reward diminishes, you have to rely more and more on your willpower.

So when you want to change something in your behaviour, it's best not to rely on willpower alone. The thing with willpower is that it's quite easy to be disciplined when you're feeling well. But there will come a time when you are tired, distracted or upset, and that's when you are most likely to slip up. If your intention is to eat less sugar, it is not wise to keep a stock of chocolate bars in the kitchen. There will always be a moment when you simply cannot resist the temptation.

The good news is that you can by-pass this willpower obstacle by cultivating a habit instead. According to Charles Duhigg, author of the book *The Power of Habit*, forming a habit is the key to successful behavioural change. Why? Because when you make a habit out of something you don't need to rely on your willpower anymore. When something becomes habitual you no longer have to go to the trouble of deciding whether you should do it or not. There's no need to weigh up the possible benefits and drawbacks each time. It is something you just do without thinking, like brushing your teeth. When was the last time you had to summon all your willpower to put your toothbrush to good use? Most people just do so without having to be extremely disciplined about it, simply because it has become a habit.

Duhigg says that you can form a habit within two to four weeks. Which is great news because it means it takes no time at all to turn something new into something you feel like you have been doing all your life. Okay, but how do you go about cultivating a new habit exactly? Duhigg bases his explanation on the principles of 'conditioning': rewarding good behaviour and punishing bad behaviour. Take raising a child, for example. If they clean their room, they will receive a compliment or some other reward. However, if they are rude to someone, you will quickly scold them.

According to Duhigg you shouldn't rely exclusively on the immediate reward that comes with your desired behaviour when forming a habit. As we have already seen, the immediate reward that comes with achieving a goal dissipates as time goes by. Instead, you should find a separate, extra reward that will serve as a source of motivation. Returning to our example of getting up earlier in the morning, you could reward yourself with an extra-long shower or an extra-tasty breakfast when you manage to rise on time. You will only need to do this for the first couple of weeks until getting up early has become a habit. After that you can reward yourself, if you like, when you manage to get up on time every morning for a whole week until eventually you don't feel the need to reward yourself at all anymore. If you reach that point, then congratulations are in order. You have just cultivated a new habit.

An alternative strategy for successful behavioural change is to aim as low as possible. One of the most common mistakes when trying to change your behaviour is setting your sights too high: 'Starting today, I'm going to run ten kilometres every morning!' Doing this means that you will only be satisfied when you deliver an exceptional performance every time. And when you fail to meet your own high expectations – which is bound to happen sooner or later – your motivation will diminish and you will lose faith in your ambitious project. A wiser move is to set goals that are so easy you cannot fail to achieve them. For example, running one kilometre three times a week. This is a surefire way of meeting your targets and reaping the resulting rewards. On good days you will probably be tempted to exceed your goal. On bad days you will still be able to achieve your goal and avoid the disappointment of failure.

Another aspect of successful goal-setting is allowing yourself some wriggle room by regarding an 80% completion rate as a successful outcome. It is impossible to succeed every single time but 80% of the time is a realistic target. An 80% success rate in terms of behavioural change actually represents a terrific outcome (without all the unwanted pressure).

In my case, I didn't quite succeed at making a habit out of getting up at 7 a.m. However, my efforts have led to me starting work before nine o'clock every morning. Well, at least 80% of the time. . .

> Choose a behaviour that you wish to change on the basis of what you have read in this book. You could pick something from your contingency plan that you would like to turn into a habit. For example, checking your e-mail less often or demanding less from yourself. Set a clear goal that can be achieved without too much trouble (e.g., not checking your mailbox between 10 a.m. and 4 p.m. two days a week) and think of a good reward for when you succeed. Keep this up for at least two weeks.

## On becoming a robot

The tips and techniques in this chapter may have given you the impression that they will only work after you have become a model of efficiency: when you can dismiss all irrelevant information from your brain, plan your working schedule perfectly, maintain a list of priorities and not devote one more second of your time to your e-mail than is strictly necessary; when you have become a robot, essentially. If this is what you are thinking right now, you may not have quite grasped the point yet. As I have just said, even if you only achieve an 80% success rate when applying the techniques in this chapter, it will result in significantly more peace of mind.

The emptier your mind, the less stress you will experience and the more time and space you will have for the stuff that really matters. However, there is one more aspect of emptying your mind that we have not yet discussed. One so important it deserves its own separate chapter: training your attention.

Empty your mind by:

- spending your time on the things that really matter and ignoring the trivial stuff;
- transferring as much as you can from your brain onto (digital) paper so that you can use your brain for the things it was designed to do;
- setting clear goals and focusing on development goals instead of performance goals;
- learning how to plan properly, create and maintain a clear overall picture and adjust your schedule when necessary;
- spending the least amount of time possible on e-mails and devising clever ways of doing so.

# 8
# FOCUSED ON THE JOB

got it from a friend of mine. He knew someone who had been given it on prescription but never used it and had decided to earn some extra pocket money by selling it on. 10mg methylphenidate hydrochloride – better known as Ritalin – in strips of ten; a medication that is often prescribed for children and adults with ADHD and sometimes also used for, let's say, different purposes. Ritalin is inexpensive and readily available, if you know the right channels. It does wonders for your concentration, keeps you alert and gives you more energy, or so it says on the box. But it's the off-label use that my students rave about because Ritalin is ideal as a performance enhancer when pulling an all-nighter cramming for an exam or for staying awake at a party. It is an amphetamine, but one that is made in a nice clean laboratory and given out on prescription. Naturally, I had to find out for myself what all the fuss was about.

After about 20 minutes I start to notice the effect of the drug. I don't feel tired anymore. My heart is beating a little faster and my breathing is more rapid. My mouth feels dry and so do my eyes. I suddenly wouldn't mind a stick of chewing gum. I have deliberately chosen a boring task for the experiment: proofreading a long piece of text. After 45 minutes I realise I am completely immersed in the task. I scroll down through the corrections like it's the most exciting thing I've ever done. I am also enjoying the monotone techno that someone recommended I should play while working. I even find myself nodding my head and tapping my fingers along to the beat.

My Ritalin-enhanced focus appears to be at its best when I am working on a well-defined task, for example editing a text or working on a new idea. When the task is more complicated, however, like when I am looking for a certain piece of information among several e-mails, I tend to lose the plot more quickly and get caught up in the details. I'm glad then that I don't have any important meetings or calls planned for today.

One hour later I have to admit I have never concentrated so well and for so long on a single task. No wandering mind, no hunger, not even a glance at my smartphone. But there are side effects, too, including increased sensitivity. I feel like I'm in a hurry and am anxious that I won't get the work finished on time. I also continue to chew incessantly on a piece of gum that lost all its flavour half an hour ago. And I feel a headache coming on. This is probably the moment when I need to take more Ritalin to prolong the effect but I decide against it. I have now experienced for myself how taking a drug can help you perform better at boring tasks. But is it really worth taking amphetamines for that purpose? Ritalin is powerful stuff, there's no denying that. It can be a great help if you have serious concentration issues, like when you suffer from

ADHD. But what about when it is used widely by people who don't really need it? How normal is that? And why are we so easily distracted nowadays that we often find ourselves turning to chemistry for help?

There is a fierce battle raging for our attention. Almost every minute of the day something is trying to grab it: messages, billboards, newspaper headlines or clickbait content. We are constantly inundated with a flood of ads, news, notifications, updates from social media and e-mail. If you live in a city, you are likely to encounter more people in a single day than most people would have met in their entire lifetime 150 years ago. There is always something going on somewhere and concentrating for any length of time in such a hyperactive world is an enormous challenge. The overwhelming number of stimuli stresses us out and exhausts us.

Still not convinced? Then have a good look around you the next time you're in the supermarket. Supermarkets are the perfect place to go if you want to witness the permanent war being waged for our attention. Every single centimetre of space is utilised to guide your eyes towards yet another new product. Large signs hang above and among the aisles announcing the latest offers. And, as if that wasn't enough, the best bargains are blared out from the overhead speakers as well. Even the temperature, lights and music are designed to manipulate you. This has become so normal that we don't even notice it anymore.

A trip to a modern-day supermarket would be absolute torture for someone from the nineteenth century. They simply wouldn't know where to look. We, however, have become so good at dealing with multiple stimuli that we can handle this kind of environment. It appears that our powers of concentration – in this case, our capacity to focus on one thing in a crowded place – have greatly improved over time. Unfortunately, the more adept we are at blocking out external stimuli, the more aggressive they appear to become. And that is why we now live in a world of pop-ups and personalised advertisements and street sellers with very aggressive sales techniques.

Given the demands being placed on our attention nowadays, it is more important than ever to know how to protect yourself from unnecessary distraction. Your attention should belong to you and no one else. In this chapter you will find a number of tips and techniques aimed at improving your powers of concentration. We will tackle the problem of notoriously persistent time wasters, take a quick course in mindfulness and discuss the philosophy behind deep work. I will also reveal my preferred technique for working with your full powers of concentration (the pomodoro technique) and share some of my favourite concentration apps with you. All of these tips and techniques will help you win the fight for your attention.

## Mindfulness

I remember it well: my very first mindfulness group. I was introduced to mindfulness meditation in college as a psychology student. Our instructor began by solemnly handing us all a single raisin. We were told to study the raisin carefully, smell it, squeeze it and then listen to it (I kid you not) and finally to eat it. This peculiar ritual took half an hour – the longest 30 minutes of my life. Time had never passed so slowly for me before. Or at least not until we were given our next assignment: to walk as slowly and as purposefully as you possibly can. What ensued was a kind of stumbling conga in which 12 self-conscious young adults tried to manoeuvre their way around a small room without falling over each other. It didn't take me long to conclude that while mindfulness may work for some people, it just wasn't my cup of tea.

However, during my research for this book I realised I would have to try to immerse myself in the world of mindfulness once again. Within 12 months I went from complete sceptic to mildly enthusiastic fan. After taking another course in mindfulness I immediately decided to sign up to become a mindfulness trainer. It wasn't all plain sailing, however. I still frequently experienced the scepticism that I recalled from my student days, especially when I had to do stuff like stand on my head against a wall to allow 'the blood to flow more easily to your pancreas.'

Mindfulness is presented as a solution for just about everything and is recommended as a treatment for all kinds of physical and mental ailments. There are mindfulness festivals, magazines, retreats, apps, kids courses and TV shows. There are even books about how your cat can teach you to 'live in the moment'. The possibilities are endless.

When was the last time you did absolutely nothing? No work, no meetings, no phone? More than a week ago? More than a month? Whereas only a few years ago mindfulness was primarily the domain of spiritual types eager to rediscover themselves (at least that's what I thought back then), it is now embraced by almost everyone. Mindfulness has become a permanent feature in the corporate sector, in health care and even in primary schools, and it is now the techies and CEOs in Silicon Valley who are leading the way in the meditation revolution. The benefits of mindfulness appear to be very real. Studies have shown that people who are adept at mindfulness techniques are happier, more empathic, friendlier, more satisfied, more independent, more optimistic and more positive than those who have had no experience with mindfulness. Practicing mindfulness is good for your self-confidence and offers protection against depression, social anxiety, worry and, of course, stress. It is also impacts your blood pressure, cortisol levels and immune system in a positive way.

Given the hectic times we live in, it is not surprising that mindfulness is gaining in popularity. We struggle daily with information overload. Our brain is always switched on. During our waking hours our focus is almost entirely externally oriented, as opposed to internally. We switch continuously from laptop to tablet to smartphone. We fill our moments of 'down time' – waiting for the train, travelling home, a half hour of peace and quiet on the couch – with even more stimuli. We do all of this simply because our brain likes to be kept busy, and these days the distraction it craves is readily available. The moments when we do nothing – moments we absolutely need as well – are becoming increasingly rare. Mindfulness offers an uncomplicated solution for the busyness in our lives. Meditation turns out to be a good way to keep your cool in the rat race. Everyone can learn how to do it. No wonder it is being heralded as the next great cure-all.

The potential benefits aside, meditation is not for everyone. This is partly because meditation isn't all sweetness and light, as some of its proponents would have us believe. In fact, it is sometimes quite the opposite. Meditation compels you to look inwards, where you will inevitably be confronted with your darker side as well: unpleasant memories, negative thoughts about yourself, the things you're ashamed of. No wonder we usually prefer doing something (anything!) else.

In a famous experiment a number of people were asked to sit alone in a room without any distractions of any kind. They had to hand over their telephone and had no access to books, newspapers or music as a form of diversion. The only thing they were allowed to do was to subject themselves to electric shocks if they wished. Almost half of the subjects chose the electrocution option over having to face the emptiness of doing nothing. And they weren't all masochists either.

It seems that many of us are a little scared of the company of our own thoughts. As Eliza said after turning to meditation in the wake of her burnout, 'Meditation isn't really chill at all because it takes a lot of effort. When I'm meditating I have to sit there in silence and try not to think, which is almost impossible because my mind is always racing. There's this constant stream of thoughts and emotions and they are mostly negative.

The trick is to try and do nothing and just feel. Just to look at the emotion and say, "God, I feel really bad" and then to accept that.'

Learning to meditate is not necessarily an easy, fun or relaxing undertaking. After all, the purpose of a mindfulness exercise isn't to make you feel relaxed. Nonetheless, mindfulness and other forms of meditation have become extremely popular. A sign, perhaps, that we are all so keen to live a more peaceful and conscientious life that we are prepared to step out of our comfort zone to achieve it.

There are plenty of books and apps you can consult if you want to find out more about mindfulness and meditation, so I will restrict myself to the basics here. To immerse yourself more deeply in mindfulness I would recommend signing up for a course with an experienced trainer.

Essentially, mindfulness is a way of meditating. It has its roots in Buddhism but in its current form it comes without the religious aspects. Mindfulness is based on two fundamental principles: 'awareness' and 'acceptance'. It is all about being aware of what goes on in your body and mind and accepting those moments when you experience tension or pain for what they are.

Mindfulness can also be described as a way of training your attention. You can use various techniques to focus your attention on yourself and keep it there for longer periods of time. This makes you more aware of what is going on inside you, both in your mind and in your body, and this is how mindfulness helps to relieve stress. You also become better at recognising signs of stress at an early stage.

During mindfulness training a distinction is drawn between the 'doing mode' and the 'being mode'. In the modern era we have become used to spending most of our time in the doing mode. We are primarily preoccupied with things that lie beyond the present moment: making progress, meeting deadlines, solving problems, getting ourselves ready for future events and reacting to external impulses. Our body may be here in the moment but our mind is usually elsewhere.

Mindfulness, on the other hand, offers us the opportunity to enter the being mode and to focus our attention on the present moment – popularly known as the 'here and now'. This is the mode in which you can be genuinely present and aware of what is going on in your mind and body. You can train yourself to enter the being mode using techniques and exercises that are aimed at keeping you in the here and now. Meditation is not the only way of entering this mode, of course. You can also take a walk in nature or (my personal favourite) go for a long drive.

Meditating also helps you to train your concentration. Exposing yourself to longer periods of emptiness and even boredom has many benefits. It helps you to connect with your own feelings, focus your attention on mundane matters for longer and deal with your own emotions and difficult moments in your life.

> For this exercise you need to sit somewhere where you have a nice view – of your garden or a quiet street, for example. Set a timer for five minutes and spend that time focusing on the view and nothing else. Try to take in as many details as you can. You will probably be distracted regularly by your thoughts

but that's okay. In fact, that is the very point of the exercise: to notice this happening so that when you become distracted you try to refocus your attention on what you had been doing. You can also try this variation: put a saucepan of water on the stove and watch it until it reaches boiling point.

Mindfulness is a skill you can train. However, the point of a mindfulness exercise is not the exercise itself but rather to train your ability to focus on the exercise. Returning to the exercise above, while doing it you were probably very aware of the stream of thoughts going through your mind and how they kept on distracting you. Were you able to retain your focus nonetheless? What kind of thoughts did you have? How did you react when you became distracted? Were you annoyed at yourself for not being able to stay focused? These exercises can be a good way of revealing your own opinion of yourself.

When you're meditating you don't have to sit in lotus position before an altar with incense burning all around you (though you may, of course, if that's your thing). Mindfulness can be practiced wherever and however you want. You don't even need to feel embarrassed about meditating at work because no one will know you are doing it (unless you start singing a mantra, perhaps). You can do it during your lunch break, in the train or even in the queue for the supermarket checkout. An easy way of getting some practice is to find a few moments each day when you can 'check in'. Take a few minutes to pay attention to what's going on in your mind and body. Notice how you're breathing, how your body feels, which thoughts and emotions you are experiencing. You can do this by yourself or with the help of a guided meditation on your smartphone.

🧍 Set a timer for ten minutes. Sit down on a comfortable chair and relax. Count to ten in your head. When you get to ten, start counting from one again. If you get distracted before you reach ten, stop and start again.

That's it. Your attention is bound to drift every now and then but that's okay. The exercise is all about training your attention.

## Deep work

One of my teachers in primary school, Mrs Peters, had a single-minded mission: to train our powers of concentration. Not one school day went by without her bringing the subject up in class. Whenever we became restless at our desks she would command us to 'Con-cen-trate!' and if you managed to spend more than half an hour focused on the assignment you were doing, Mrs Peters would make sure to pay you a compliment. She obviously believed that you could train your concentration and the sooner you learned how to do that the better.

Back in my early school days there were no mobile telephones in the classroom and the internet could only be accessed through a loudly beeping modem. Twenty-five years later I often find myself wishing I still had Mrs Peters around to help me concentrate because I am so easily distracted by external stimuli. And during those rare moments when I am fully focused, I always have a long list of other things-to-do fighting for my attention. Things that are all far easier than writing a book, for example. Not surprisingly, when I was writing this book I had to cut myself off regularly from the outside world by disappearing to a cottage – one without internet – in the middle of nowhere for a few days.

It's rather unfortunate that it costs us so much effort to concentrate for any length of time. After all, we do our best work when we can focus our attention on a task or problem for longer periods. That is precisely when we come up with brilliant ideas. The ability to concentrate intensely on something difficult is very important, particularly to an employer who appreciates you being able to dive into a complex problem and stay there (which can apply to everything from writing an elegant piece of computer code to drawing up an excellent business plan).

In his book *Deep Work* computer scientist Cal Newport suggests that we ought to reassess our ability to concentrate. Deep work refers to the ability to concentrate on a complex task for a long period of time. If you have ever become so wrapped up in something that you experienced a kind of 'hyper focus' and were able to shut out the outside world, then you know what deep work means. According to Cal Newport, it is this way of working that leads to brilliant ideas, increased productivity and a deep sense of satisfaction in your own work. It usually takes an hour of intense working to reach a state of deep work. And that's when you start making real progress.

Unfortunately, very few of us are able to manage 60 consecutive minutes of intense work these days, as sustained concentration is fast becoming a scarce commodity in the modern working environment. We are becoming experts at 'shallow work' – the opposite of deep work – in which our work is carried out mainly at the surface level: replying to e-mails, attending meetings, talking to colleagues and ticking off the tasks on our to-do list. Newport is concerned about the current imbalance between shallow work and deep work. A large part of our working day now consists of rapid, superficial tasks. Tasks that we sometimes try to bundle together through multitasking, for example by replying quickly to a few e-mails on your laptop during a meeting or conducting a telephone conversation while scanning a document at the same time. This kind of multitasking may make us feel like we are being very productive but the reality is quite different. Doing two things at the same time usually takes you longer than when you do them separately. And the results of your efforts are often poorer in comparison.

The more shallow work you do, the less time there is for deep work. Of course, it doesn't help that deep work often involves such complex tasks that we are sometimes afraid of tackling them and even end up avoiding deep work altogether. It requires intense effort and, like long-distance running, the first 20 minutes can be really tough going. Sometimes you have to endure a non-productive hour of work before you reach a state of flow. It is a far easier (and often more appealing) option to continue replying to your e-mails than to settle down to work on a complicated and important task. This will sound familiar to anyone who has ever experienced the sudden urge to start tidying up their desk while attempting to work on a crucial assignment.

Applying yourself fully to a task is quite difficult. As a result, deep work is often ignored in favour of shallow work, which is significantly easier. And this is a shame, says Newport, because it is during your deep work time that you can really make a difference and prove your worth. Your shallow work abilities will not distinguish you from your colleagues and peers, as everyone is good at shallow work. You will only ever make a real difference through the things you accomplish during periods of deep concentration and when you are prepared to put in the required effort. Careers are built on deep work, not shallow.

You can train your capacity for deep work, but it does require some exertion. Newport suggests that we all give ourselves the gift of a deep work self-training programme. Begin by marking off moments in your week (90-minute blocks) during which you can work without disruption on a sizeable and complicated task. This means finding a place to work where no one can interrupt you (avoid your open-plan office in other words!). A set of noise-reduction headphones that filter out ambient noise can also help to shut out the outside world. Make sure your smartphone is out of sight and switched to silent mode and close your e-mail. Keep in mind that it may take between ten and thirty minutes (or even longer) to reach a state of flow. Also, stick to the start and end times that you have assigned to the task. You can dedicate all the time you like to your shallow work before and after the slot you have allocated for your deep work.

It can help to carry out your deep work at a location other than where you do your shallow work. This will act as a kind of signal to yourself that you are going to concentrate on a single task. In his book Newport gives examples of people who disappear to a cabin in the woods or use the train or airplane for their deep work. But it can also be helpful when you simply decide to sit at a different desk from where you usually sit.

Newport recommends only doing this a few times a week in the first few weeks of your deep work training programme. Deep work can be extremely intensive, especially if you are used to multitasking and tend to dedicate most of your time to shallow work. At first you will probably feel inclined to revert back to simpler tasks purely because they are easier to do. But despite how difficult it may be initially, try to stick with the programme. Honing your deep work skills takes both time and effort but pretty soon you will notice a difference and feel able to take on a few hours of deep work every day.

Separating your deep work from your shallow work is an excellent way of making your working day more productive. It also helps with regard to stress levels because it shows you how to maintain your concentration during deep work, secure in the knowledge that you will get your shallow work done on time as well.

For the coming week, schedule two 90-minute blocks for deep work on an important project or task. Follow the instructions above and make sure no one can disturb you. Dedicate all of the allocated time solely to the task in question (while at the same time allowing for some possible frustration). Afterwards, assess what it was like to work in this manner and how satisfied you are with the results.

## The pomodoro method

This book was written almost entirely in 'pomodoros'. The pomodoro technique allows you to divide your working day up into a predictable pattern of concentrated working punctuated by regular pauses. It provides motivation, makes you more satisfied with your work and helps to make even the largest tasks more doable. And all it involves is setting an alarm. I just love pomodoros.

The trick is to divide your day up into 25-minute blocks of concentrated work, each one followed by a 5-minute period of rest. The blocks are called pomodoros and you can fit quite a lot of them into a normal working day. Pomodoros are particularly good for tasks that require a few hours of work, such as editing copy, writing a report or studying for an exam. As a method it is both spectacularly simple and extremely effective.

It works like this: pick a task and schedule a few hours in your diary for working on it. When you are ready to start working, set an alarm for 25 minutes. Spend those 25 minutes on the task and nothing else. When the alarm goes off take a 5-minute break (set an alarm for this too!) to do whatever you like: check your WhatsApp, search for memes on Reddit, stare out the window. When the alarm goes off again to signal the end of the break settle down to another 25 minutes of work, followed by another five-minute break. When you have done this four times in succession, take a 15-minute break. Repeat ad infinitum or until you reach the end of your working day.

This method works so well because 25 minutes is a perfectly manageable period of time. During that time you don't have to worry about the size and complexity of the overall task. You only have to focus on the next 25 minutes and they will have flown by before you know it. This helps you to make your time more quantifiable, to be satisfied with your work regardless of the final result and to be happy at the end of the day, even if you don't get everything finished: 'Okay, it would have been nice to get more done, but I got through eight pomodoros today, so kudos to me.' This technique also makes sure you take enough breaks, which is very important in terms of your motivation. The prospect of 25 minutes of concentrated effort is doable and you can leave anything else that pops up in the meantime until later ('I'll be taking a break in ten minutes so I'll deal with it then').

After you have been using the pomodoro technique for a while you will probably start thinking in terms of pomodoros, too ('I'm going to need two pomodoros for the next job'). This can give your working day a more regular rhythm. When I was writing this book I managed to fill ten pomodoros with intensive writing each day. All extra writing time after that was a bonus. When I only had half a day free to write I filled five pomodoros and never felt like I had come up short, even when I didn't get the chapter finished. And if I really didn't feel like working any more after eight pomodoros, the prospect of 'only two more pomodoros' kept me going.

Working in pomodoros allows you to evaluate yourself in terms of the effort you put in and not your performance.

And it does wonders for your motivation. But where did the name come from, I hear you ask? The creator of the technique had an alarm in the shape of a tomato. . .

> Tomorrow, divide your day into pomodoros. Work in a concentrated manner in cycles of 25 minutes followed by a five-minute pause. Take a longer break after completing four cycles. Analyse what the technique does for your motivation and efficiency.

## From source of stress to source of solace

Sometimes help comes from the most unexpected places. Our mobile phone, so often a source of stress and distraction in our lives, can also help us to improve our concentration. In recent years, numerous apps have appeared on the market offering us better powers of concentration and improved organisational abilities. Many useful mindfulness apps have been launched, too. Below are a few of my favourites; apps that I have been using over the past few years to create more peace and calm and boost my concentration.

Our smartphones have native apps that track your smartphone usage and provide you with a daily update. In iOS this is called 'Screen time'; Android calls it 'Digital Wellbeing'.

These apps keep a record of your usage in the form of graphs and statistics, which was how I discovered that I reach for my phone around 40 times a day and spend 60 to 90 minutes using it. I was flabbergasted. To make matters worse, at the weekend I sometimes spend as much as four hours a day glued to my smartphone. Four hours! No point in trying to deny the obvious when you're confronted with this kind of hard data. Thankfully, smartphones also offer ways of limiting your screen time to a specified number of minutes per day.

Willpower is overrated, that much became clear in the previous chapter. I for one found out that I needed real help to break my habit of checking Facebook at every available opportunity. Ultimately I decided to remove Facebook from my smartphone, but that wasn't enough. I simply switched to spending more time on my computer to scroll through the endless series of cute cat videos on my timeline. I was saved in the end by a browser extension called **WasteMyTime**. It works like a child lock by blocking heavily-used time wasters (Facebook, Reddit, 9GAG). When you navigate to one of these sites, you are directed instead to an alternative website that asks you, 'Shouldn't you be working?' Of course, this doesn't stop me from using a different browser to visit those sites if I want to, but that requires a more complex action on my part. Instead of relying on a well-worn automatism, I now have to go out of my way to get my Facebook fix, something I am far less likely to do.

**Be Focused** is an app that helps you to work in pomodoros. There is an app for your smartphone and also one for your computer. I prefer the desktop version. You can use it to set a timer that counts down from 25 minutes. When you have reached the end of a pomodoro an alarm goes off (it's pretty loud, so it's wise to deactivate it if you are working in a quiet place, like a library). Another timer keeps track of your breaks. In other words, it does exactly what it's supposed to do.

There are also many apps that offer breathing exercises. The app **Oak** is useful for the 4-7-8 technique because it does all the counting for you. The **Breathing App** is more minimalistic: a ball on the screen grows and shrinks as you inhale and exhale.

To be honest, there are so many mindfulness apps that it's almost impossible to choose between them. I haven't tested them all (when it comes to apps it is usually better to be a satisficer and not a maximiser), but out of those that I have tried I would recommend **Headspace**. It offers a number of easy-to-do meditation exercises. The free basic programme has ten guided meditations ranging from three to ten minutes in length. The app also explains the basics of mindfulness using video clips and the narrator has a pleasant British accent.

My favourite app of all is called **Forest**. This app can help you to concentrate by stopping you from reaching for your smartphone every single time you receive a notification. I like Forest because it makes very clever use of human psychology. The app works on the basis of a very simple principle. You set the timer in Forest for a specific number of minutes. During that time a tree begins to grow in the app. If you keep your hands off your phone for the duration of that period, a beautiful tree appears in your virtual garden. However, if you can't resist the temptation to sneak a peek at your other apps, your tree will die. And of course no one wants their tree to die! Failure to comply, however, will result in a dead tree standing in your virtual garden for all eternity – a sad reminder of the moment when you just couldn't control yourself. So when you have Forest on board you might think twice before reaching for your phone at every available opportunity. An app that makes you feel guilty about your smartphone usage – sheer genius if you ask me.

All of these apps are available in the Apple and Google app stores and while the above list of productivity apps is by no means exhaustive, it should give you an idea of what's out there. Of course, some of these apps may have become obsolete by the time this book makes it into your hands, but there are always new ones ready to take up the baton. The best thing is to do a bit of window shopping yourself.

## Your attention is yours alone

In the busy and demanding times we live in, your attention is actually a kind of superpower. But unlike many superheroes, to harness that power you don't have to drink a radioactive magic potion or spend years training with a grumpy monk high in the mountains of Nepal. Improving your powers of concentration is something that can be done at home and at work. Training your attention – for example by learning how to meditate – is not always easy, but the results can be amazing. Now is the time to reclaim your attention from everyone and everything that has been trying to steal it. Remember, your attention is yours and yours alone, so be careful with it and try not to give it away so easily again!

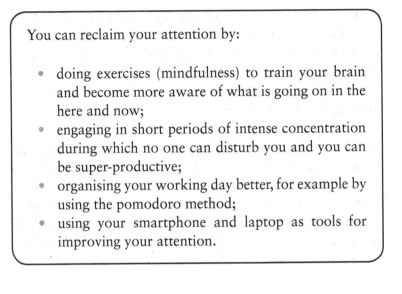

You can reclaim your attention by:

- doing exercises (mindfulness) to train your brain and become more aware of what is going on in the here and now;
- engaging in short periods of intense concentration during which no one can disturb you and you can be super-productive;
- organising your working day better, for example by using the pomodoro method;
- using your smartphone and laptop as tools for improving your attention.

# 2030 BURNOUT-FREE – A MANIFESTO

You have already read in this book that I regard being busy as a choice. And you have read how stress works and what causes it. You've also learned what you can do to combat stress and bring more peace and calm into your life. The message up to this point has been that it is *you and you alone* who can reduce your stress levels.

That is not the full story, however. Stress is a problem that affects and involves us all. We are all responsible for pushing each other to live faster, fuller and more intense lives, with ever-rising burnout numbers as a direct result. Moreover, it doesn't look like our professional lives are going to become any less busy in the foreseeable future – and the same applies to our personal lives, too. In fact, with technology advancing at breakneck speed, our work is demanding more and more from us and our diaries are bursting at the seams like never before. The pace of modern life is becoming faster and the tools we use to remain 'switched on' are only going to multiply.

A worrying percentage of the population is already being affected by burnout. This applies to people of all ages, but the figures are highest for those who are just embarking on their professional careers. And the most recent tragic trend is the rising number of high school students who are crumbling under the pressure to perform and suffering from burnout.

Things are going to have to change. Each burnout is one too many, not only because of the cost to society but particularly because of the amount of suffering it causes and the enormous waste of talent. We can reduce the number of burnouts when we start recognising that it is not a problem for the individual alone but one that we all must help to solve.

I have a dream: to beat the current burnout epidemic by the year 2030. Coincidentally, I also have a slogan: 2030 BURNOUT-FREE. But why 2030? Because it gives us just under eight years to change the way we live, which should be plenty. We can call a halt to our crazy busy lives and help everyone (including ourselves) to avoid the trials of a burnout. But this dream can only become a reality if we all pitch in. So, starting today, it's all hands on deck!

We need to lift the taboo that surrounds stress and burnout. It is high time that we stopped regarding people who suffer from stress as weak and feeble and instead applaud them for listening to what their body is telling them. We have to stop viewing stress as something that is 'all in your head'. We need to acknowledge the fact that it can make you very ill and that too much stress can have serious consequences for your health in the long term. Ultimately, we want to arrive at a situation in which this has become such an accepted fact that our first instinct when we are under too much stress will be to take our foot off the pedal – by calling in sick, for example – in order to prevent things from getting worse.

We also need to invest in an early warning system. People who are stressed often don't realise it themselves and it is those closest to them who usually end up sounding the alarm. In organisations, managers, doctors, teachers and HR personnel should be taught how to recognise signs of stress and how to address them. Reducing the number of burnouts will also require new legislation that protects people from stress at work.

This chapter contains a number of suggestions on how to make 2030 BURNOUT-FREE a reality. There are also some tips on what you can do when you are worried about someone who is struggling with stress and how to reduce stress at your place of work, particularly when you are a manager or employer. The chapter finishes with a few suggestions on how we can tackle stress, both at the political level and as a society. 2030 BURNOUT-FREE will require us to change the way we think about being busy. We need to take (drastic) steps to improve the situation. We have a duty to protect our own health and that of others, too. It won't be easy but it is certainly possible, as long as we are all willing to do our share.

2030 BURNOUT-FREE? YES WE CAN!

## When you are worried about someone

After reading this book you will (hopefully) be better able to handle the stress in your own life. However, you may also be worried about someone you suspect is heading straight down the burnout road. It may even be the reason why you bought this book in the first place.

Let's get the bad news out of the way first: no matter how much you want to, you cannot solve other people's problems for them. You cannot decide for someone else whether they need help or not, that is something they must do themselves. Furthermore, the health and well-being of another grown-up is never your responsibility. No matter how well intentioned it may be, unsolicited advice almost always falls on deaf ears. It can even lead to resistance or irritation: 'Mind your own business!'

However, this does not mean you have no choice but to stand back and watch while someone rushes headlong into a burnout. There are plenty of ways you can offer support. One thing that often helps is talking to the person about your own experiences with stress, just to get the conversation going. Seeing that you are vulnerable, too, helps to lower their guard and acts as a signal that it is safe for them to discuss their feelings with you. Often the best way to help someone is simply by setting a good example.

Another way to start the required conversation is by asking open questions about how they deal with pressure. Simple, neutral questions like 'You're awfully busy, aren't you?' or 'What do you do when you're feeling stressed?' can create the kind of opening that encourages the other person to speak freely.

If you are very worried about someone, it may help to share your concerns with them. Make sure you do this tactfully and avoid making the other person feel like they are doing something wrong. The best approach is to speak about your observations in the first person: 'I've noticed recently that you have been [. . .] and I get the impression you're under a lot of stress. Am I right?'

Expect also to meet some resistance. After all, you are inter-fering in how someone is living their life and they won't always thank you for that (at first). You will most likely be dealing with a person whose basic stress level is very high. They could quickly accuse you of meddling in their affairs (which, let's face it, you are). Indeed, they may even get angry with you before taking your advice to heart at a later date. So make sure you're not too pushy; if the other person makes it clear that they do not appreciate your comments, just let it go. It is not your job to 'save' them.

As we have already seen, people tend to look after others bet-ter than they do themselves. And this makes it even more important that we keep a close eye on each other – family, friends, work colleagues – and to offer help if and when it is required (as opposed to forcing it upon them).

## At work

We are prepared to go to great lengths for the sake of our work, even at the expense of our own health. At the same time our jobs are constantly demanding more from us. We also let our work impinge regularly on our free time and we end up doing more and more overtime, often without even getting paid for it.

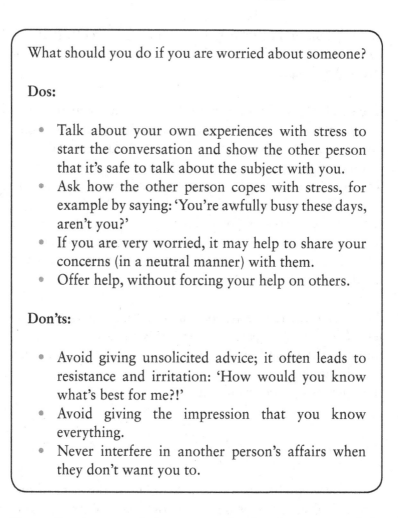

What should you do if you are worried about someone?

**Dos:**

- Talk about your own experiences with stress to start the conversation and show the other person that it's safe to talk about the subject with you.
- Ask how the other person copes with stress, for example by saying: 'You're awfully busy these days, aren't you?'
- If you are very worried, it may help to share your concerns (in a neutral manner) with them.
- Offer help, without forcing your help on others.

**Don'ts:**

- Avoid giving unsolicited advice; it often leads to resistance and irritation: 'How would you know what's best for me?!'
- Avoid giving the impression that you know everything.
- Never interfere in another person's affairs when they don't want you to.

Up until quite recently it was completely taboo to complain about stress at work. You could be labelled as 'weak' if you were apparently unable to cope with the pressure. Unfortunately, this is still the case within some organisations, where employees who are prepared to work themselves to the bone often receive the most praise. There are still plenty of companies where unhealthy working behaviour is regarded as a sign of 'commitment' and even earns you brownie points.

The winds of change have started blowing, however, and an increasing number of organisations are now paying more attention to stress and burnout. Sometimes this happens out of necessity, like when a number of employees in a department fall victim to burnout or when even the manager can't take the heat anymore. Staffing shortages often force companies to invest in mental health, if only to ensure that they control the outflow of personnel. More and more organisations are also beginning to acknowledge that a happy workforce translates into a more productive workforce. They appear to have finally read the memo that says that when you look after your employees they will be worth more to you in the long run, and that if you treat your workers instead like disposable items, you will inevitably end up with a continuous stream of burnouts.

If we want to be burnout-free by 2030, many aspects of the way we work will also have to change. We need to make major progress on improving the well-being and sustainable employability of workers. In concrete terms this requires organisations to do the following: make stress a topic of discussion, teach workers the basics of stress reduction and take measures to reduce the levels of stress on the work floor.

You don't necessarily have to occupy a management position to be able to bring about the required change. You can achieve a lot just by setting a good example for your colleagues. Bring the matter up in meetings and offer suggestions on how working conditions could be improved. Do not underestimate the impact you can make by sharing your own experiences with stress. It may even encourage others to open up about their own struggles. It will also help to foster understanding and show that preventing burnout is a shared responsibility.

If this topic is not high on your manager's agenda, you may have to take the initiative yourself and explain to them that investing in burnout prevention can reap rich rewards. Point out that the productivity of workers who suffer from excessive stress tends to drop dramatically and that this is often a completely avoidable situation.

Once stress has become a topic of conversation you can get down to the business of reducing it. There are many ways of creating a stress-free working environment. As an example of low-hanging fruit, you could consider adjusting the means of communication: which applications will be used to send which kinds of messages and at which moments in time? For example, you could agree to use the telephone only for urgent communications and never for non-urgent matters. Agree also that it is perfectly fine to reply to e-mails and apps the next day instead of immediately. Decide when it is okay to disturb someone for work-related matters outside of office hours. It will save everyone a lot of headaches when you can switch off your work telephone at the end of the day and not feel obliged to keep track of your e-mail, Slack or WhatsApp messages.

Other areas that can be addressed include overtime and what to do in the event of an absent colleague. How much overtime is acceptable to you as a team? What can the team do to prevent the burden from falling on the shoulders of the most 'responsible' team member? How should overtime be rewarded? To what extent do you have the right to refuse to do overtime if it doesn't suit you? And if someone cannot come in to work, is the rest of the team responsible for taking up the slack or can you recruit external personnel for the job?

As a manager or team leader you are partly responsible for reducing and preventing stress in your team. The most obvious ways of doing so include making (new) employees more stress resistant by offering them courses on how to deal with stress and employing a coach to whom employees can turn for help when they are feeling the pressure.

Make sure you are able to recognise early signs of stress in your team. A person who is suffering from stress may fail to realise it themselves, as stress ironically often creates a blind spot that makes you less conscious of your own stressed-out behaviour. They may even insist that everything is fine. Keep your finger on the pulse and trust your own instincts. Is someone in your team acting more irritated than usual? Then you should address the matter with them in a nonthreatening manner. Make sure they have immediate access to a company doctor if they are displaying symptoms of burnout. Also, keep abreast of the protocols regarding burnout and make sure you know how to reintegrate someone who is recovering from a burnout. You should be aware, for example, that people returning to work after a burnout often tend to overexert themselves when they resume their responsibilities, so you may have to slow things down a bit for them at first.

There are steps you can take with regard to working conditions that may help to reduce stress levels. For example, by making healthy food available, discouraging staff from eating their lunch at their desks and encouraging them to go for a walk during their break. Hold meetings for 55 minutes instead of the standard 60, so your team can take a minute or two to organise their thoughts before plunging into the next meeting. It is small steps like these that can really make a difference. Offering mindfulness courses is also a good way of tackling stress. Some organisations even provide their employees with in-house courses and group meditation sessions.

We can only really start to reduce stress levels when we change working conditions to suit the worker, not the other way around, and doing this should be a team effort. I was recently given an excellent example of how this should be done. A doctor was finishing her first day of work at a new clinic. When her shift ended she sat down at her desk to do some administrative work and update her files, like she had always done in her previous job. One of her new colleagues came over to her and said, 'I'm sorry to disturb you, but I see you're still working after your shift has ended. To avoid unnecessary stress, we as a team have an agreement: no one is to work outside of their normal hours. We feel it's in everyone's best interests. So could you please finish this tomorrow?'

## Drastic measures

No matter how important it is to take good care of the people around you and to improve the working conditions of your team wherever you can, this often only addresses the symptoms of stress without tackling its root causes. Tackling stress at the source – and achieving our 2030 BURNOUT-FREE

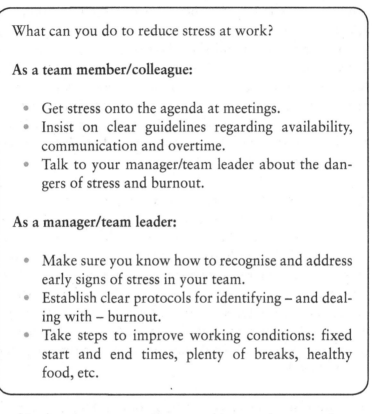

What can you do to reduce stress at work?

**As a team member/colleague:**

- Get stress onto the agenda at meetings.
- Insist on clear guidelines regarding availability, communication and overtime.
- Talk to your manager/team leader about the dangers of stress and burnout.

**As a manager/team leader:**

- Make sure you know how to recognise and address early signs of stress in your team.
- Establish clear protocols for identifying – and dealing with – burnout.
- Take steps to improve working conditions: fixed start and end times, plenty of breaks, healthy food, etc.

goal in the process – requires something much more substantial: culture change.

The importance of getting enough rest has long been recognised in the world of professional sport. Recently, I was given the opportunity to talk to a few professional athletes about their training regimes. I had always imagined the schedule of an athlete preparing for the Olympic Games to be chockfull of intensive training sessions. Turns out this is only part of the story. One of the most important elements of any Olympic training schedule is getting plenty of rest and relaxation. An athlete who fails to recover properly will end up pushing themselves too hard and runs the risk of 'overtraining', the equivalent of burnout in the professional sporting world. Regardless of how fit you are, overtraining can result in you peaking too soon and prevent you from performing at your best when you need to. That's why a professional athlete's schedule contains not only intense effort but plenty of rest days, sleep and healthy food, too.

What applies to top athletes also applies to the rest of us: if you expect to be able to perform regularly at your peak, you must get enough rest. Like professional athletes, we can only handle the daily marathon we call 'work' if we also afford ourselves enough recovery time. Nevertheless, most of us tend to fill the gaps in our diaries with work and other activities instead of leaving some room for rest and recuperation. And to make matters worse, when we do take some time off we often feel guilty about doing nothing and not putting our time to 'good use'.

If we want stress and burnout to become a thing of the past, we will first have to remove the taboo that surrounds getting enough rest. Moments of rest and relaxation ought to occupy a more prominent place in our lives. These important moments should not be regarded as a kind of 'breather' in between jobs but as a natural and fundamental part of our way of life. Rest is actually crucial to our well-being and is good for both body and mind. We all need at least a little time to think, to reflect on life and even just to be bored. All of which is impossible as long as we continue running flat out on the treadmill.

We need to relearn the art of rest, especially in these hectic times. I like to imagine that in a few years from now it will be entirely acceptable to say, 'Given how hard I worked last week on our project, this week I am going to take a day off.' Getting enough rest is not just something we should do when we are exhausted. We need to see it as crucial time that we use to build up our reserves. At school the mantra should not only be that you have to do your very best every day, but also that you can only perform at your peak when you are adequately rested. It is only when we fully embrace rest that we will be able to take a stand against stress and burnout.

Burnout is a serious problem, one that our politicians need to start taking seriously. Given the high costs attached to burnout and the serious consequences for those affected, something has to be done to reduce the number of stress-related complaints at work. This involves not only supporting those who suffer from burnout, but also placing burnout prevention higher on the agenda.

In her book *Willing Slaves* (2004) Madeleine Bunting makes a case for what she refers to as 'the politics of wellbeing': policies that are aimed not only at supporting economic growth but also at securing the rights of workers. Bunting proposes a number of measures[9] that would help to reduce stress, especially among those who have caring responsibilities in addition to their work. Among those measures are:

- The right to flexible working, which can only be refused on the basis of a strong business case.
- Universal childcare for all three and four-year-olds.

- A care allowance for parents caring full-time for children under the age of three.
- A universal state pension which compensates for breaks in employment to provide care.

Today, after 18 years of massive technological advances, I believe we should add the following measures to Bunting's original list:

- The right to switch off your work telephone in the evenings and at the weekend without any fear of negative consequences.
- The right not to be disturbed during your free time by work-related e-mails and messages.
- The availability of coaching and/or support in the case of work-related stress, so that steps can be taken before someone reaches the point of burnout.

There are a number of experiments currently being carried out in different places around the world to examine the feasibility of a four-day instead of a five-day working week. The results to date have been very promising. The productivity of workers does not appear to fall. They are happier, more relaxed, and more focused in their work. It seems that when you have less time to do the same amount of work, you become much better at setting priorities. Reason enough, perhaps, to abandon the 40-hour working week in favour of a 35 or even a 32-hour version.

The aforementioned measures could be combined with the kind of legislation that is already in place in France, where firms and organisations employing more than 50 people are prohibited from sending e-mails to their workers during non-working hours. This would free workers from the responsibility to monitor their work-related messages in their down time after their shift has finished and during the weekend. Another step would be to require employers to make a greater financial contribution to covering the costs of illness and absence caused by work-related stress. This would also encourage employers to take the complaints of their workers in relation to stress more seriously.

I am not naive, however, and I do not expect these kinds of measures to be welcomed everywhere with open arms. Working groups will first have to be set up and covenants signed. Negotiations will have to take place between employers and workers and some sacred cows will have to be sacrificed. Whatever happens, the alternative is far less attractive: that we all fall prey to even more stress in the future.

## Two scenarios

It is difficult to predict how things will be in 2030. By then the human race will undoubtedly have made huge leaps forward, for better or for worse. Technology will have developed exponentially and smart, self-driving electric cars may have finally put an end to traffic congestion. And at home we may spend most of our evenings in the realm of full-body VR simulations. Who knows? In any event, 2030 is a lot closer than you might think and the things we do and the choices we make today are going to influence the shape of things tomorrow. With regard to stress, there are two scenarios to choose from.

In the first scenario for 2030, we will be subject to an even more demanding labour market characterised by little security and a lot of risk. We will have created technology that will tighten its grip on us even further. We will end up spending every 'unproductive' minute of our time submerged in a world of likes, technostress and the crushing pressure to perform. We will work non-stop and fill the few moments of free time we are given to the brim with entertainment and activity. Instead of living, we will be 'lived', and at an increasingly faster pace, too. Absenteeism arising from stress will be the order of the day and the percentage of burnouts will rise and rise.

In the second scenario we will have embraced the concept of rest as an important aspect of our lives. It will be possible to combine a full-time job with caring responsibilities and self-development. We will be encouraged to look after ourselves and there will be enough help available for dealing with stress. We will use technology to stay connected to others but will not allow it to dictate our lives. The percentage of burnouts will be negligible. This is what the 2030 BURNOUT-FREE dreamworld looks like.

It is up to us to choose between these two scenarios. Will we remain slaves to our work or will we opt for a better balance between work and leisure? Do we want to continue living in a world of likes or will we protect ourselves from the terror of social media? Will we try to keep up with a rapidly accelerating world or will we set the pace ourselves? Will we choose to live or be lived?

The choice is ours. And we must make it, otherwise it will be made for us.

We can be BURNOUT-FREE by 2030 but that demands action: on the personal and professional level, and on a much larger scale, too. We can only achieve this goal when we start taking our health more seriously than we have done up to this point.

And that is something we can start doing today.

# THE DARK ARTS OF STRESS RELIEF

Below is a list of the most important insights in this book condensed into one-sentence snippets. I like to refer to them collectively as 'the dark arts of stress relief', but if that sounds a bit too sinister you can file them under 'words of wisdom for a more peaceful life'. Together they form the principle ideas in this book. The list may prove useful in times of need, so hang it up in a prominent place at home and at work so that it can act as a kind of reminder every now and then.

- Stress is unavoidable but being busy is a choice.
- If you work during your free time, it's not free time.
- You are not obliged to reply to an e-mail just because someone decided to send it to you.
- E-mail is a to-do list for you that is managed by others.
- Your time and attention are your most important assets. Use them wisely.
- Missing out is unavoidable but it is not something we need to be afraid of.
- Finding the Ultimate Option – if there even is such a thing – is rarely a worthwhile investment of your time.
- If you don't choose how to live your life, someone else will do it for you.

- There are very few things that need to be perfect.
- You are probably less indispensable than you think (which is good news).
- A little tension can be a good thing but being subjected to too much stress for too long is bad for your health.
- When you are stressed you become pretty good at fighting and fleeing but not so good at thinking straight.
- Burnout is like an emergency brake for the body, an injury to the stress system.
- We are not just some kind of walking brain; there is a whole body attached, too.
- Stress is always accompanied by warning signs that differ per individual. You should be aware of your own warning signs.
- Your head is not designed for storing stuff; that should be done elsewhere.
- You can reduce stress by setting development goals for yourself instead of performance goals.
- If you don't set priorities, everything becomes a priority (and so nothing gets prioritised).
- Sometimes the most important things are the least urgent and sometimes the most urgent things are of no importance at all.
- The key to forming a habit is to set an easy goal, reward success and stick at it for at least a couple of weeks.
- A more peaceful life requires a good balance between doing and being.
- The ability to concentrate is the most valuable skill in modern-day work.
- Work is a marathon, not a sprint.

# References

## Introduction

CBS Statline (2018). *Psychosociale arbeidsbelasting (PSA) werknemers; geslacht en leeftijd.* statline.cbs.nl

TNO (2014). *Factsheet werkstress.* www.monitorarbeid.tno.nl/publicaties/factsheet-werkstress

## 1 We're All Workaholics Now

Acton, A. (2017). *How to stop wasting 2.5 hours on email every day.* www.forbes.com

Chui, M., Manyika, J., Bughin, J., Dobbs, R., Roxburgh, C., Sarrazin, H., Sands, G. & Westergren, M. (2012). *The social economy: Unlocking value and productivity through social technologies.* McKinsey Global Institute.

De Botton, A. (2010). *The pleasures and sorrows of work.* Emblem Editions.

Keynes, J. (1930). *Economic possibilities for our grandchildren.* Entropy Conservationists.

Kushlev, K. & Dunn, E. W. (2015). Checking email less frequently reduces stress. *Computers in human behavior,* 43, 220–228.

Morris, D. Z. (2017, 1 January). New French law bars work email after hours. www.fortune.com

TNO & CBS (2013). *Nationale enquête arbeidsomstandigheden.* www.monitorarbeid.tno.nl/nea

TNO (2017). *Onbetaald overwerk in Nederland.*

Smith, A. P., Johal, S. S., Wadsworth, E. J. K., Davey Smith, G., Harvey, I. & Peters, T. (1998). The Bristol stress and health at work study: The questionnaire and results from the pilot study. *Occupational Health Review-London, 75,* 11–13.

Verhaeghe, P. (2015). *Autoriteit.* De Bezige Bij.

## 2   Always in a Hurry

Alexander, B. K., Beyerstein, B. L., Hadaway, P. F. & Coambs, R. B. (1981). Effect of early and later colony housing on oral ingestion of morphine in rats. *Pharmacology Biochemistry and Behavior, 15*(4), 571–576.

Asano, E. (2017). *Social media today: How much time do people spend on social media?* Socialmediatoday.com

Bakhuys Roozeboom, F. (2018, 16 March). We zitten opgesloten in de wurggreep van WhatsApp. *NRC.*

Brickman, P. & Campbell, D. T. (1971). Hedonic relativism and planning the good society. In M. H. Appley (Ed.), *Adaptation-level theory* (pp. 287–305). New York: Academic Press.

Chernev, A., Böckenholt, U. & Goodman, J. (2015). Choice overload: A conceptual review and meta-analysis. *Journal of Consumer Psychology, 25*(2), 333–358.

Clayton, R. B., Leshner, G. & Almond, A. (2015). The extended iSelf: The impact of iPhone separation on cognition, emotion, and physiology. *Journal of Computer-Mediated Communication, 20*(2), 119–135.

Dijksterhuis, A. (2015). *Op naar geluk: De psychologie van een fijn leven.* Prometheus.

Ferriss, T. (presenter, 2018, 4 January). How to handle information overwhelm #289 [Podcast]. *The Tim Ferriss Show.*

Godin, S. (2018). *The difference between time and money.* www.sethgodin.com

Kramer, A., Westermann, E. & Launspach, T. (2017). *Het Millennial Manifest: een nieuwe kijk op keuzestress, prestatiedruk en verbondenheid.* Valkhof Pers.

Rushkoff, D. (2013). *Present shock: When everything happens now.* Penguin.

Schwartz, B. (2004, January). *The paradox of choice: Why more is less.* Ecco.

Schwartz, B., Ward, A., Monterosso, J., Lyubomirsky, S., White, K. & Lehman, D. R. (2002). Maximizing versus satisficing: Happiness is a matter of choice. *Journal of personality and social psychology,* 83(5), 1178.

# 3 Being Busy is a Choice

Burka, J. B. & Yuen, L. M. (1983). *Procrastination: Why you do it and what to do about it.* Perseus Books.

Curran, T. & Hill, A. P. (2017). Perfectionism is increasing overtime: A meta-analysis of birth cohort differences from 1989 to 2016. *Psychological Bulletin.*

Jellison, J. M. & Green, J. (1981). A self-presentation approach to the fundamental attribution error: The norm of internality. *Journal of Personality and Social Psychology,* 40(4), 643.

Latané, B., Williams, K. & Harkins, S. (1979). Many hands make light the work: The causes and consequences of social loafing. *Journal of Personality and Social Psychology,* 37(6), 822.

Ruggeri, A. (2018). The dangerous downside of perfectionism. *BBC Future*

Smith, M. M., Saklofske, D. H., Yan, G. & Sherry, S. B. (2017). Does perfectionism predict depression, anxiety, stress, and life satisfaction after controlling for neuroticism? *Journal of Individual Differences,* 38, 63–70.

Tracy, B. (2007). *Eat that frog!: 21 great ways to stop procrastinating and get more done in less time.* Berrett-Koehler Publishers.

Urban, T. (2013, 30 October). *Why procrastinators procrastinate.* www.waitbutwhy.com

# 4 Your Boss is a Bear

De Vente, W. (2011). *Sick and tired: Psychological and physiological aspects of work-related stress (thesis)*. Faculty of Social and Behavioural Sciences (FMG) en Faculty of Medicine (AMC-UvA), Amsterdam.

Disalvo, D. (2017). *How Breathing Calms Your Brain, And Other Science-Based Benefits Of Controlled Breathing*. Forbes Online.

Kalat, J. W. (2015). *Biological psychology*. Nelson Education.

McEwen, B. S. (2005). Stressed or stressed out: what is the difference? *Journal of Psychiatry and Neuroscience*, 30(5), 315.

Miller, T. W. (1989). *Stressful life events*. International Universities Press, Inc.

Palahniuk, C. (2005). *Fight Club: A novel*. WW Norton & Company.

Segerstrom, S. C. & Miller, G. E. (2004). Psychological stress and the human immune system: a meta-analytic study of 30 years of inquiry. *Psychological Bulletin*, 130(4), 601.

Harvard Health Publishing (2018). *Understanding the stress response*. www.health.harvard.edu

# 5 Burnout

De Wachter, D. (2012). *Borderline Times: Het einde van de normaliteit*. Lannoo.

Keller, A., Litzelman, K., Wisk, L. E., Maddox, T., Cheng, E. R., Creswell, P. D. & Witt, W. P. (2012). Does the perception that stress affects health matter? The association with health and mortality. *Health Psychology*, 31(5), 677.

Kirsch, Dr Daniel L (2019, May 28). *Burnout is now an official medical condition*. www.stress.org

Launspach, T., Van der Deijl, M., Spiering, M., Heemskerk, M. M., Maas, E. N. & Marckelbach, D. (2016). Choice overload and the quarterlife phase: Do higher educated quarterlifers experience more stress? *Journal of Psychological and Educational Research*, 24(2), 7.

Schaufeli, W. B., Leiter, M. P. & Maslach, C. (2009). Burnout: 35 years of research and practice. *Career Development International,* 14(3), 204–220.

Segerstrom, S. C. & Miller, G. E. (2004). Psychological stress and the human immune system: A meta-analytic study of 30 years of inquiry. *Psychological Bulletin,* 130(4), 601.

Wester, J. (2017). *Kosten van burn-out bedragen 60.000 euro.* NRC.

# 6 Warning!

Brehm, J. W. & Cohen, A. R. (1962). *Explorations in cognitive dissonance.* John Wiley & Sons Inc.

MacDonald, G. & Leary, M. R. (2005). Why does social exclusion hurt? The relationship between social and physical pain. *Psychological bulletin,* 131(2), 202.

Pang, A. S-K. (2016). *Rest: Why You Get More Done When You Work Less.* Basic Books.

Peterson, J. B. (2018). *12 Rules for life: An antidote to chaos.* Random House.

Salmon, P. (2001). Effects of physical exercise on anxiety, depression, and sensitivity to stress: A unifying theory. *Clinical Psychology Review,* 21(1), 33–61.

Tuk, M. A., Trampe, D. & Warlop, L. (2011). Inhibitory spillover: Increased urination urgency facilitates impulse control in unrelated domains. *Psychological Science,* 22(5), 627–633.

# 7 Peace of Mind

Allen, D. (2015). Getting things done: The art of stress-free productivity. Penguin.

Covey, S. R. (1991). The 7 habits of highly effective people. Simon & Schuster.

Duhigg, C. (2012). The power of habit: Why we do what we do in life and business. Random House.

# References

Pareto, V. (1906). *Manuale di economia politica* (Vol. 13). Societa Editrice.

Urban, T. (2018, 11 April). *How to pick a career (that actually suits you)*. www.waitbutwhy.com

## 8 Focused on the Job

Cirillo, F. (2006). *The pomodoro technique (the pomodoro)*. Agile Processes, 54(2).

Kabat-Zinn, J. (2003). Mindfulness-based interventions in context: past, present, and future. *Clinical psychology: Science and Practice,* 10(2), 144–156.

Kabat-Zinn, J. (2009). *Wherever you go, there you are: Mindfulness meditation in everyday life*. Hachette Books.

Keng, S. L., Smoski, M. J. & Robins, C. J. (2011). Effects of mindfulness on psychological health: A review of empirical studies. *Clinical Psychology Review,* 31(6), 1041–1056.

Newport, C. (2016). *Deep work: Rules for focused success in a distracted world*. Hachette Books.

Wilson, T. D., Reinhard, D. A., Westgate, E. C., Gilbert, D. T., Ellerbeck, N., Hahn, C., Brown, C. L. & Shaked, A. (2014). Just think: The challenges of the disengaged mind. *Science,* 345(6192), 75–77.

## 2030 Burnout-free – A Manifesto

Bunting, M. (2004). *Willing slaves: How the overwork culture is ruling our lives*. HarperCollins.

# Notes

1. In the past, management roles were primarily filled by males. Thankfully that has since changed!
2. One way to circumvent the above problem is to use the excellent website 'Let Me Google That For You', which finds the relevant Google search results for your query and sends them in an e-mail.
3. An elevator pitch is a brief speech no longer than the duration of an elevator ride: the amount of time an important person will give you to pitch your product.
4. It should be pointed out that this is based on correlational research from which no cause and effect relationship can be deduced.
5. You are under no obligation to explain your decision to the other party. But if you do decide to offer an explanation, regard it as a service and not as a duty. And if you don't want to offer any reasons, just remember: *'no' is a complete sentence.*
6. *Burnout syndrome* first appeared as an 'occupational phenomenon' in the WHO's *International Classification of Diseases* (ICD-11) in 2019. Burnout is not granted the same status, however, in the DSM, the diagnostic manual for psychiatrists and psychologists but is listed instead as an 'adjustment disorder'.
7. A word of caution. I am not a medical doctor and I don't want to create the impression that I'm an expert on the human physical condition because I'm definitely not.

The symptoms I describe here can have causes other than stress. So if you are worried about any of these symptoms, my advice is to visit your GP.

8. I've not invented this exercise. It's an adaptation of a story told by Stephen Covey.
9. Despite the fact that Bunting's book was published over 18 years ago, the measures she proposes are still valid today. Unfortunately, this also means that we have made little progress on safeguarding the well-being of workers in the intervening 18 years. . .

# Index

Page numbers followed by *f* and *t* refer to figures and tables, respectively.

good reasons for, 55
and having to vs.
wanting to, 57–60
mindfulness as
uncomplicated
solution for, 189
minimising effect of, xi
perceived as good, ix
and perfectionism,
69–75, 70*f*, 75*f*
and procrastination, 64–68
and sense of responsibility,
75–81

Calm, 52. *See also*
Peace of mind
Canceling appointments,
xx, 142
Career, as identity, 6–9
Caring:
for others, 207–209
for yourself, xv–xvi, 135
Change(s):
with apps, from sources of
stress to sources of
solace, 200–203
for becoming burnout-free,
212–214
in behaviour, 175–179 (*See
also* Habits)
in educational system,
10–11

in nature of work,
3–4, 10–12
in priorities, 166
to reduce stress, 136–147
Choice(s), xiv
being busy as a, 53 (*See
also* Busy-ness)
of more relaxed life, 86–87
(*See also* Peace of mind)
power of, 56
Choice overload, 38–42
Coaches, modern
managers as, 13–14
Cognitive dissonance, 134
Cognitive loops, 48–51
Cognitive symptoms of
stress, 138*t*, 140
Commitment demanded by
work, 12–16
Communication:
about another person's
stress, 208–210
always-on, 16–20, 47
changing language you
use, 59–60
drawbacks of
e-mail, 20–25
indications of attribution
style in, 59
saying "no," 81–86
senders and receivers
in, 82–84

# Index

portrayals of success and
happiness in, 31–32
Meditation, 186–193
Memory, 155–156
Mental health, determinants
of, 136
Mind:
body–mind connection,
135–136
body–mind disconnection,
124–125
and choice overload,
39–40
cognitive loops, 48–51
efficiency and productivity
of, 152–153
emptying your, xvii–xviii,
155–158 (*See also*
Peace of mind)
focusing your (*see* Training
your attention)
in the knowledge economy,
4–5
overloaded, 143
thinking differently, 56
Mindfulness, 186–193
apps for, 200, 202
benefits of, 188
and meditation, 186–193
organisational
courses for, 214
simple exercise for, xx

in training attention and
concentration, 190–193
Mobile phones, *see*
Smartphones
Multitasking, 21–22, 195

Nature of work, changes in,
3–4, 10–12
Need to switch off, 25
Nervous system, 92–93
Newport, Cal, 153, 194–197
"No," saying, 81–86
Nothing, doing, xx
Notifications:
brain's response to, 45–46
turning off, xvii, 48

Oak, 202
Occupation, as identity,
6–9
Others:
critical attitude toward
performance of,
69–70
worry about, 207–209
Overclocking, 34–38
Overload(s):
of activity, 31
of choices, 38–42
information, 188
of our minds, 143
Overtime, 212–213

# Index